"**You Are Love** is a modern hero's journey — a courageous exploration into unknown territory, in which obstacles are overcome, wisdom is gained, and the hero returns to share hard-earned lessons. The spiritual insights which Sudeep Balain has gained will encourage anyone who aspires to deeper meaning and greater fulfillment in life."

—Larry Dossey, MD
Author: *ONE MIND: How Our Individual Mind Is Part of a Greater Consciousness and Why It Matters*

You Are Love

You Are Love

A True Story of Self-Transformation

Sudeep Balain

ISBN: 1519399456
ISBN 13: 9781519399458
Library of Congress Control Number: 2015919398
CreateSpace Independent Publishing Platform
North Charleston, South Carolina

Once I scrubbed myself clean within,
I discovered I was love.
So are you.

Just like a butterfly transforms from an
egg to a caterpillar to a pupa and then to its
incredible beautiful self, so are we evolving and
transforming ourselves, knowingly or unknowingly,
through our daily living.

Contents

Acknowledgments

THIS BOOK IS dedicated to my mom and dad, Prem Devi Balain and Dr. K. S. Balain, who brought me to life in this world in India, a land of great ancient wisdom. Thanks to Mother India for everything it has freely nourished my soul with over the years. Thanks to my three beautiful, soulful children, Rohan, Arkin, and Samara, for deciding to come on another earth adventure together so we can mutually keep learning and growing in spirit. And thanks to Sunaina, their mom, for being my toughest teacher this time around.

I have come to realize that our self-realization is only possible via our daily relationships and our learning from them. So thanks to all my friends who came in and out of my life at just the right times to help me continue to propel my spiritual flowering forward. Thanks also to all those I encountered in my life who never opened the door in spite of my many knockings. Had they done so, I wouldn't be here writing this book. Everything happens just as it's meant to.

I want to thank my dear daughter, Samara, who is all of fourteen, for taking the photo I use on my author's page toward the end of the book.

Lastly, I want to thank from the bottom of my heart all the beings of light of the spirit world, who continue to guide me on this incredible human journey of mine.

Introduction

THIS IS A true story of my self-transformation—physical, mental, emotional, and spiritual. I have come to understand and realize through the direct experience of living my life of the past almost ten years that the less conditioned I became through my own self-efforts, the happier, more peaceful, and less conflicted I felt.

As I felt happier within, I stopped smoking cigars, ate better, didn't feel the need to drink alcohol, lost close to thirteen pounds, and was brimming with excess energy daily. I also dropped my waist size from a thirty-three to thirty-one. I realized firsthand that I had an emotional relationship with food. Spiritually, I became much more connected with myself and everyone around me and started to realize the oneness and equality of all humanity. I realized that what is sacred in me is also sacred in you, dear reader—that at the core, at the root level, we are not two but one. I started hugging more. This is my story. This is also your story.

Intellectually, I knew all this before I got started. But as I went through the self-purification process, I came to understand that going from my head to my heart (i.e., actually living such a life) was the real work that enabled me to break free from my habits I was stuck in, and that brought about real, lasting change in my behavior and response patterns in my daily living.

Also, if I didn't reduce my conditioning, my conflicts within to start with, whatever else I tried to build on top of that shaky foundation could never produce lasting results. I had been on enough yoga retreats and visits to Hawaii to know that the bliss and glow that percolated because of these visits soon dissipated once I got back into my regular rhythm of daily living. I first had to self-clean and empty out what was not good in me (i.e., what was not serving me anymore). This is why I have spent the majority of my effort and time in the book on ways to achieve this self-cleaning. What follows is automatic. As we start cleaning ourselves from within, the love and happiness and our compassion and kindness toward ourselves and others simply shows up. I had to make no effort to try to be nice or humble; that was my original nature. It was almost like as I cleaned my garbage within, the treasure underneath was simply waiting to be discovered in me, within each of us. Our primordial nature is that of peace, love, harmony, sharing, and empathy toward one and all.

I also realized that to begin this process of self-purification or self-cleansing, I had to stop pointing my finger at the world as a cause of my everyday problems and start pointing it toward myself. My process in earnest could not start, I realized, till I did that. That was the first major shift I had to make in my thinking process, that I alone am the cause of my unhappiness or happiness. I am in full control of my destiny via my actions.

As we embark on this short journey together, I ask you to please stay receptive to what I offer in the book. Keep an open mind and an open heart to see where this book takes you.

As far back as I can remember, I have always been curious and open to all the mysteries of our world, especially of the spirit kind. Being more right-brained, I have always enjoyed exploring our subjective world that seems to be constantly ebbing and flowing with unseen energy, seemingly connected to everything and everyone.

I had often wondered how mediums connect with the other side. Clearly, this phenomenon of mediumship was not a hoax; so many proven good mediums over our human history have been able to give very precise psychic readings, and some even showed the much rarer physical-materialization gifts of people long dead. I had also read a lot about the capabilities of some of the most gifted and tuned-in psychic mediums, like the British Ena Twigg, Betty Shine, Ivy Northage, Helen Duncan, and Alec Harris, among many others.

I had heard that astrologers in India, some really good, could potentially map out my future. How were they able to see my future, and if my future had already occurred in some dimension, what was the purpose of my life?

It had also become pretty apparent to me through my experiences that often, in spite of my best efforts, the doors that I really wanted to open never did. As an example I clearly remember the time when I was still working on Wall Street in 2002. Twice I got opportunities to work at a large and successful hedge-fund group as a senior research analyst with one of its most profitable technology teams. Both times, over the span of almost three years, it didn't work out. Once, it seemed I had asked for too much money, and the other time, they decided to hire a younger guy instead. Fast-forward some years later and the fund was embroiled in one of the many insider-trading scandals that rocked Wall Street.

Another example happened in early 2006 when I really wanted my marriage to stay together, but in spite of my best efforts, it was not meant to. I tried and tried, but it was all in vain. In hindsight, had my divorce not gone through, I most likely wouldn't be here writing this book.

I am grateful now for all the doors that never opened, indicating to me that I was simply not supposed to go that way. Did this mean that my life was being guided by someone or something? Why was it that certain doors would open at just the right time, often effortlessly, and not others? I often wondered such questions aloud among friends. All I got were puzzled looks and some lame answers. Nobody I knew seemed to care enough to find out.

I had heard through a friend about this really good medium in San Francisco, and out of mere curiosity, decided to pay him a visit. My father had passed away in March 2008, and I wanted to see if Felix, this medium, could connect me with him. While there, for fun I wanted him to tell me what he saw for my future as he peered into it, which I knew good psychics could do. "What could be the harm?" I thought. Worst case, he would be wrong. So what—worth the experience anyway. This has always been my outlook on such matters.

It was September 12, 2013, around 2:35 p.m., and I found myself sitting in Felix's office. It had taken over two months to get in to see him.

My father did come. So did my father's older brother Surat, also in spirit. I did not see either of them but communicated with them via Felix. Some of the information shared was pretty personal and precise, things Felix would not have known.

During the one-hour session, Felix suddenly asked me, "So where is your book? I have never come across anyone like you."

Unprepared, I said, "What do you mean?"

Felix added, "I have never come across anyone who went through what you have gone through and came out the other end looking as good as you do. You need to share your story."

I mentioned that I planned to, but I just wasn't fully cooked yet.

He smiled and before moving on added, "I see you sharing knowledge material with lots of people in group settings. I see you presenting stuff to people. Do you do presentations now?"

This book is my attempt to lay open and share my journey of self-transformation—physical, mental, emotional, and spiritual—over the past almost ten years, initiated by my rather difficult divorce against my deep wishes in early 2006. In hindsight that personal, very difficult setback was the best gift I could have asked for, as it started my deep journey of self-awareness and full examination of who I was, eventually leading to my self-transformation and realization.

I am a pretty deep person by nature in the sense that if I like something, I go as deep as I need to fully understand the process at hand so that I am eventually, through my research and investigations, able to put my arms around it. Then as it becomes a part of my being, I automatically release it and move on.

From my personal setback, my divorce, this innate desire took over, and I wanted to understand whether there was a coherent framework to the functioning of our lives, and if so, what was it? Did the yogis and sages of ancient India who wrote the Vedas, the mighty *Upanishads*, the *Bhagavad Gita*, and the *Yoga Vasistha* know the answers? And if so does it tally with what science has been discovering along the way? As I went further, related questions kept coming up: Is there life after death? If so, what is it like? If we are mean, petty, small-minded, and selfish in our conduct in this life, does the same personality continue in the afterlife as well, or is there a chance for a full cleanse and restart? If not, shouldn't we be living a gentler and mindful daily life of love, peace, and compassion toward one and all? Can we accrue merit, and should we try as we go along? Does my learning as an entity ever end?

Over the course of the next almost ten years and counting, from 2006 on, I studied—not read and leafed through, but actually deeply studied—each of the over two hundred different spiritual books of all genres and natures. This list is mentioned in sequential order toward the end of the book. I have also mentioned the dates that I began and finished each book. As you will see, some books are easier reads than others. No matter. I kept plowing through them. It is also very interesting how I was almost guided to read one book after the next. It is still fascinating to me to see how I got from one to the next. It is almost like everything in life is weaved in a certain pattern on our tapestry and the discovering and unweaving of it is simply the unfolding of our lives.

As I was doing my MBA here in the United States in 1987 and 1988, my first passion of reading and learning became marketing, sales, and management books. I loved them and ended up working in Silicon Valley in marketing at technology companies for ten years after finishing my MBA.

The next passion I discovered for myself was Wall Street. This was 1999, and the market was booming. Like so many others, I was enthralled by this rising surf. Money seemed to be so easy to make. What a racket. I started picking stock, mostly making money as the market just kept climbing, almost uninterrupted, and had been since 1982. What I did not know (nor did anyone else, it seemed) was that the peak of this huge bull run was at hand over the next year. But more than the money, the whole seemingly unpredictable nature of the market (which was human beings in the end) took me in. Human nature had always intrigued me. Why do we behave the way we often do? Why are habits so difficult to break for most of us if we know or at least believe that we have free will?

I took a big pay cut and an even bigger demotion in position and started as a research associate from a director-of-marketing-level position in this new adventure. Now mind you, there is nothing lower than a research associate position in a Wall Street research firm. Luckily, my job demanded a thorough understanding of the companies I was to research and the technical merits of their products, so I was at home. I just had to learn how Wall Street functioned. Again, my thirst for knowledge and my curiosity drove me to read Wall Street books written by or about all sorts of legends, new and old. I read about the great Jesse Livermore who had made and then lost a fortune many times over and eventually killed himself. Wall Street history is full of legends like this. I read about Soros and Buffett and everyone in between to better understand the game being played.

In hindsight, my third and last frontier of adventure was being initiated right before my eyes via my divorce in early

2006 and would potentially give me another great opportunity of learning and growth. It was as if my spirit guides were again opening a new door of learning and growth for me. I did not realize it then, but this learning and growth had no ending. It continues in the here and the hereafter. All this I came to fully understand much later.

I clearly was not seeing it this way in early 2006, as I was mired in all my pain, anger, and frustrations. As the famous poet and mystic Kahlil Gibran said in his best-selling book, *The Prophet*, "Your pain is the breaking of the shell that encloses your understanding."[1] This deep pain comes into our lives in different forms, often as a loss of a loved one or a divorce that one doesn't want or expect, as was my case.

I am a life coach now and tell people, including my clients, that when such deep pain shows up in our lives, the key is to not run away from it but to bear it with all the love and tolerance within. It is easier said than done. This is, in my own experience, the best way to dissolve it over time. If we keep running away from pain (or fear or any other deep-seated emotion), it simply follows us around like a shadow in our potential relationships and life. Its intensity never truly leaves us.

As the fog of pain started to ebb and clear away due to my continued processing of it in real time, somewhere around 2008, I started to see what an amazing opportunity was at hand for the personal learning, growth, and evolution of my consciousness. As more time has gone by, today, and every day over the past many years, I continue to feel so lucky that I was able to accelerate and enhance my personal spiritual growth via my personal setback. Had I not gone through all I did, I wouldn't be here writing this book that might potentially help shed light on similar personal learning, healing, and growth for my fellow human beings.

When I was starting out in 2006, I didn't know what to read, how to cleanse my conditioning, or even what conditioning was, for that matter. I was mostly steeped in the material world, too busy to pay much attention to what was within me that needed constant cultivation. My earnest hope in writing this book is that if you are going through any kind of personal change or contemplating, or even questioning, a need for personal change and growth, this book can help and guide you because my journey is also your journey.

Our life's journey in the end is, in roundabout ways, simply about transcending our ego so we can experience God as love directly within. Often we resist, deny, or try to circumvent, but life catches us again and again and tries to hammer home this basic idea of our need to learn to transcend our egos. We eventually start listening and realize that the sooner we start listening to what life is trying to teach us via our daily experiences, the faster we can get to the end by simply learning to start letting go early and often. The more we keep resisting where life is trying to take us, the more friction (and stress) we end up creating for ourselves and those around us, resulting in more wear and tear on our bodies, minds, and spirits.

Overall I have tried to keep the text as tight as possible around my relevant experiences and thoughts at the time I was experiencing them. For me less has always been more. So many of our spiritual experiences can't be fully put in words; frankly, they lose their intensity each time one tries to elucidate them. The sweet water of love simply resides at the bottom of each of us, waiting patiently to be tasted. It is covered by our ignorance, our egos. Until the structure of our ego is understood and thus transcended, we can't get to this water, this God or love within. Thus in my experience, much of the purpose of our religious, ritual, and spiritual work is only to dissolve this conditioning within, to transcend this ego of ours. Once we do that via whichever way we choose, we automatically become one with God within. It's really that simple, and hard.

I also got to learn that on our individual spiritual growth, maturity, and eventual flowering, there are no shortcuts or easy ways, at least in my experience. We each have to do our individual work depending on our level of spiritual growth coming into this (and each) life and simply pick up from where we left off last time. How do we know how far we reached last time? Simply pick up whatever religious, ritual, or spiritual practice you feel comfortable with in the here and now. Start there. All paths are leading to the same place within us in self-realization, in oneness with God within and without. If we look with an open mind, this is so. It matters not if you are not religious, if you are an atheist or agnostic. The same process is working for each of us. We are children of that same energy or consciousness that some of us also call God in its various forms and beliefs.

Is it possible then to find this kingdom of God within us in this lifetime? Absolutely! God to me is unconditional love within each of us.

Living and functioning in our three-dimensional reality of space and time, the closest we can come to experiencing God is our own self-realization, our becoming one within ourselves when ego is transcended. Some of the expressions of this same experience over our history are, "The kingdom of God is within you," "I became God," or "I and God are one." This experience of oneness within is a full and complete realization that what I have been searching for is who I actually am. I am that. Then it is no longer an intellectual understanding and expression of what God is. Then we know via our own direct experience, and such an experience, if authentic, completely transforms us as a person. In this experience of our oneness within, we become love and are completely transformed for everyone to see. The attributes of this love are ecstasy, bliss, a state of underlying perpetual happiness, an innate knowing that we are all connected and one, humility, compassion, kindness, and a desire to help and selflessly serve whomever we encounter in our daily lives via our circle of interaction. We deeply realize that we are all spiritual beings having a human experience.

You Are Love

One no longer only defines, describes, or identifies oneself as Christian, Jew, or Hindu or as black, white, gay, or straight. We transcend such societal and often self-created mental human barriers. We are now in way deeper waters within. If we went a couple of miles deep into the earth without a tracking device, I am sure it would be hard to tell where India, Russia, or Peru is. Man-made outer definitions and boundaries give way. We discover that at the root level, we are all the same, and the innateness of this humanness is love that keeps us bound together in spite of all our apparent surface differences. This is my direct experience in my self-realization and the experience of so many others over time and human history. All the self-realized beings of light have said the same thing, that the real purpose of our lives is to make this connection with God or love within, in the here and now.

Then one becomes a servant of this love and only desires to help one and all achieve that same state. Then one does not "try" to be compassionate or kind or sympathetic; we realize we are that. And this love that unceasingly continues to well up from within us is nonpossessive, unconditional, and choiceless toward one and all. And the more of this love we give to others, the more we receive and experience it within. We realize then that this is the true nature of each of the seven billion-plus human beings inhabiting the earth today. Each of us is this unconditional love only.

Sudeep Balain

Butterflies, with their abundant and sheer beauty of colors, have always reminded me of their lightness, happiness, gentleness, and freedom. They are also a great example of nature's process of self-transformation at work, as it moves from egg to caterpillar to pupa to itself in its incredible natural process of metamorphosis. Human self-transformation, or our process of self-realization, in my mind, is also a similar experience whereby we get to transform ourselves daily to a newer, much more improved version of ourselves with dedication and self-effort. This is the true purpose of our lives.

When I read a book, I end up developing an interactive real-time connection with what I am reading in the book, such that I often take small notes when necessary. This has proven to be very useful now that I am writing this book and trying to reflect on times long gone. Once I finish a book, I have a habit of also writing down the dates of when I started and finished it. This is how I was able to come up with the list of books offered in the appendix for you to use on your personal journey if needed. Lastly, I also write down my overall impression of the book once I am done. I started doing all of this from the start of my spiritual journey for two reasons. The first was really for my kids, Rohan, Arkin, and Samara, so that as they grow up and inevitably get caught in the ups and downs of life and decide to see what Dad was reading at any given point, there would be a ready source of inspiration and reading material to help them navigate through it. The second was so I could also trace back my emotional and spiritual development over time. I wanted to be able to see how I was transforming. What I was reading and how I was expressing myself through each book via my handwritten notes could also give me a glimpse of my actual transformation in slow motion, if such a thing is indeed possible.

The real purpose of reading all the books we do is so that we are better able to understand how to read the most important book of all, ourselves. Our whole spiritual journey is simply about that. As Jesus said in *The Gospel According to Thomas*, "Whoever knows the All but fails to know himself lacks everything."[2]

I have also included in the appendix a list of movies I watched that were very helpful in opening my heart and increasing my deeper understanding of myself and continued flowering.

Lastly in the appendix, you will also find a list of sayings and observations. These can be used as tools to go deeper within for reflection and contemplation. To stay centered during my daily ups and downs, I often read my favorite ones and then close my eyes and sit in meditation for ten to fifteen minutes twice a day. This helps me dissolve my daily accumulated conditioning. Play with them, and see what works for you.

In fact, the whole book can be used as a meditation exercise in self-reflection and introspection. Just stop where you find a writing that resonates with you, and close your eyes for ten to fifteen minutes as you gently reflect on what resonates within you. You will see yourself sinking deeper in self-understanding. The deeper you go, the more you will release. The more you release, the happier and freer you will feel.

Part of the ancient India tradition of learning and spiritual-wisdom partaking has an inbuilt sense of utmost respect and compassion for all teachers one encounters on his or her journey. They can be teachers from our early-childhood schools to our engineering schools of higher learning, and they can be the wisdom and yoga teachers one learns from and encounters along the way. Teachers were, and still are for the most part, held in such high esteem as an equal stature to one's parents. That is how I have looked at all the teachers I have learned from thus far, and this is why as you go through the book, I have patiently tried to mention and recall how each of the teachers I have encountered continue to propel me further. I thank them from the bottom of my heart.

Since we are all at different stages of our personal growth and transformation, this book can be read and assimilated at different levels of our depth. Leave for now to revisit later the stuff that you find dense or with which you can't seem to agree. You will notice that over time, as you keep going deeper within yourself, more of what I have written in the book will become more acceptable to you.

This book is a string of my life experiences of the past almost ten years. It is my true story.

Part One: Growing Up in India

Sudeep Balain

I WAS BORN in a small village, Mehlana, about six kilometers from Sonipat, a town right off the highway and about an hour out of Delhi heading toward Chandigarh in the northern part of India. My father, having returned from the United States with a PhD in physics from Louisiana State University (LSU), Baton Rouge, was working in Pilani, in the state of Rajasthan. My childhood was happy and typical of kids at that time, mostly spent playing and hanging around with friends all day. I grew up in an unorthodox Hindu household. I don't remember my mother actually going to a temple, but we had a small temple inside and outside the house in Pilani and one inside the house in Chandigarh, the city we moved to in 1975, when I was twelve years old. I remember growing up in Chandigarh listening to Pink Floyd, Led Zeppelin, and Eric Clapton. Later, while studying engineering at college, I was transfixed by Ayn Rand and the intensity and single-mindedness of her books' characters.

My father was an *Arya Samaji* and passed away in 2008 at the age of seventy-nine. Before we touch on Arya Samaj, let me say a few words about Hinduism and the Vedas and their utter significance in our modern daily living.

Hinduism traditionally has been more a way of righteous living and conduct than a religion in my mind. Vedas are the oldest Hindu texts dating, some say, to over 3000 BCE. The earliest Vedic proponents keenly observed that change was inherent in human living and that it is this constant change in our lives that causes suffering. Since change appeared to be inevitable in daily living, the goal from earliest times in ancient India has been to understand suffering, its chief causes and potential remedies.

Often in our daily lives, we try to deal with suffering by overindulging in our consumption of food, alcohol, drugs, money, and our ever-increasing daily distractions. We also try to control change in our lives, mostly without much success and lots of resultant aggravation. Either way, we soon realize that in spite of our abuse of alcohol, food, or drugs, suffering can't and won't leave us till it is fully understood and thus transcended.

All this the great Indian sage Buddha knew well over twenty-five hundred years ago, from his own keen daily observations, and thus he based his four Noble Truths principally on the causes and cessation of suffering itself.

Because suffering is so predominant in our daily human living, happiness stays fleeting and ephemeral. This too the Vedic yogis observed keenly. Thus the goal of all Vedantic texts and commentaries from earliest of times has been to focus on ways and means to discover and prolong our human states of happiness, contentment, and peace.

What was found after repeated daily yogic, so-called experiments through their deep introspection and meditations, was that human happiness can only be maintained and prolonged through our state of equanimity, and equanimity can only be had through our detached fulfillment of necessary daily activities or duties.

This then is one of the important and basic messages of *The Upanishads* and the *Bhagavad Gita*, the two primary texts of Vedanta that we will explore in more detail later in the book.

Hinduism then is all about discovering and prolonging our states of happiness, peace, and bliss through right conduct in daily living. The end goal of such a human life is *Samadhi*, our self-realization.

Arya Samaj, or Noble Society, is an Indian religious reform movement founded by Swami Dayananda in 1875. He was a *sanyasi* (renunciant) who promoted the Vedas instead of idol worship as a way to connect with the higher Reality within and without. His Vedic schools put an emphasis on Vedic values of belief in one God, right action and conduct, of selfless service, and compassion toward one and all.

These Vedic Schools represented the first practical application of Dayanand's vision of religious and social reform, which was based on Vedic tradition. At these Vedic schools, students were not allowed to perform traditional idol worship, or *murti puja*, and were instead expected to perform *sandhya* (a form of meditative prayer using Vedic mantras). I remember my dad's oldest brother, Sis Ram, in our village doing this meditative practice every evening after his bath, when we used to visit the village during our summer vacations while living in Chandigarh.

My mother, on the other hand, used to worship (and still does) God via his various manifestations, such as Laxmi, Ganesh, Hanuman, and Shiva. Hindus overall believe in one formless God, Brahman, who is manifested in different genders, names, and forms all over the country.

A typical weekend day at the Arya Samaj Temple, which I remember visiting only a couple of times in my youth, would consist of a sermon given by a knowledgeable visiting householder from society. There are no priests, if I recall, in an Arya Samaj Temple, only local householder members who take turns running the non-profit temple organization. The upkeep of the temple finances is via money donations by members of the temple itself and some outsiders. This setup is very different from a typical Hindu temple that is oriented around an idol and its worship. Some of the famous Indian temples in the South have many billions of dollars' worth of gold received as donations by people at large.

My parents were not religious per se, and I grew up in a pretty open-minded environment. The focus, at least from my father's side, was on reading the ancient wisdom scriptures of the Vedas, *The Upanishads*, and the *Gita*. As I recall, all was inclusive as far as faith was concerned. I had been to a church many times in Bangalore, *Gurdawaras* (Sikh temples), and of course to

Hindu temples, and I also remember visiting the temple of the Bhai faith in Delhi.

In hindsight it was this openness toward all religions during my childhood years that helped me to investigate, with full passion and fervor, the religious and spiritual traditions of the world religions much later in my life in the United States.

Part Two: Looking for Firmer Ground—Tiburon

Years of 2006 and 2007

Sudeep Balain

By 2006, AFTER living in Westport, Connecticut, for three years and working on Wall Street in Manhattan all this time, we were ready to move back to sunny California. We decided to live in Marin and ended up buying a rather large house in Tiburon. The house was six thousand square feet and overlooked the ocean, with perfect views of the water and San Francisco. We thought it was time to lay down our roots. By then I had quit working with the New York-based hedge-fund group I had worked with for two years and started my own business in late 2005.

Well, as we all know, when we least expect it, life has a way of throwing us a big curve ball. My marriage by then was like most other marriages I knew. We'd been married for sixteen-plus years, shared three small kids, and I was trying to get my own small hedge fund off the ground, a rather intense effort in its own right.

After being served divorce papers in early February 2006, and once the initial shock of what lay in front of me settled, I decided to call one of my best friends, my dad, from India to come stay with me for a bit. The goal, with the support and feedback from my parents in India, was to see if my wife and I could learn from what precipitated the divorce filing and try to patch things up. I also figured with my dad there, together we would be better able to cope with this quickly unraveling situation that was completely out of my control now that lawyers were involved on both sides. Working on Wall Street for many years, both on the buy and sell side, and before that in Silicon

Valley in technology companies, I was used to being in client situations that often got unruly, but I knew how to contain the damage and often was able to guide them to mutually successful endings.

This was completely different and new for me—I was not in charge. I remember telling a friend that I felt like I had tripped on a double black diamond ski trail, lost control, and was just sliding down the mountain with nothing solid I could hold onto. It was a new and scary feeling. It felt, for the first time in my life, like I had no solid ground underneath me anymore. It was as if someone had pulled the carpet from underneath me and everything I had worked so hard to build the past twenty years of my life in the United States was unraveling completely out of my control.

In the meantime my dad, while staying with me in April 2006, started slipping into a depression, apparently triggered by the news of my divorce. Two weeks after he'd arrived in Tiburon, I had to take him to see a psychiatrist. Suddenly, instead of him helping and supporting me, my new role was to start taking care of his emotional wellness and upkeep. My kids were small. My oldest, Rohan, was eight, and the twins, Arkin and Samara, were only five. They clearly were also coping with immense change, living in two homes and being witnesses to the back-and-forth between their parents. I knew this new situation with my father was not tenable, and I had to send him back to India after about eight weeks with me.

I remember one of the biggest frustrations I had to deal with was that my lawyer and I pretty much had no control over the speed of the divorce proceedings. My thought by then was that since we were going to go through this divorce, let's settle it as soon as possible and move forward. But the other side often had different intentions. Often we would go to court and already be in front of the mediation judge, and the other side would show up unprepared, so very little would get done, and it would be a waste of time and money. The game being played was to endlessly tire me so I would settle for the best possible outcome for the other side. The other side, of course, was my wife, whom I still loved. This is what happens when expensive lawyers get involved on both sides. Nobody wins, and both parties lose, except the lawyers of course. This whole divorce rigmarole was proving to be quite a new learning experience for me.

This limbo state lasted for all of 2006 and the early part of 2007. By then I had shut down my fund, as I simply couldn't concentrate on work. Once I put my dad back on the plane to India, I realized that I had almost no one to talk to at a deeper level to help me ease my anger, grief, and frustration. I tried a psychiatrist but found that experience not particularly useful. Maybe I just didn't encounter the right therapist at the time. Most of our friends, except a few, were simply not interested in dealing with me and my new problems. I had a friend in Charan who still lived in Tiburon, along with his wife, Sylvia and they often insisted I join them for dinner at their home, which I frequently did alone or with my children. In hindsight those visits acted as such a soothing balm on my injured psyche. I had another close school friend in Abhinav, a prominent lawyer in Delhi. We were childhood friends since seventh grade in Chandigarh. We would often talk on the phone, and he helped me as much as he could from afar.

On my first trip back to India with my kids, during the summer of 2006, he introduced me to their family astrologer, Mr. Sharma. I had never been to one and was open to understanding what the heck was going on in my life—why me?—and any help was most welcome at that stage of my confusion. I was simply struggling to cope with life and its relentless unfolding. The astrologer asked for my date, place, and time of birth. Since I was born in a village and at home, my mom and all my relatives had conveniently forgotten my exact time of birth. Nobody records exact birth times in Indian villages. The closest I got out of my mom was that it was late in the afternoon. Mr. Sharma, based on my date, place of birth, late-afternoon time frame, and number of siblings, figured the most probable time of my birth to be three thirty. With that, it was easy for him to make a *Patri*, or astrological chart, for me. On my next visit, after a week or so and at about $400, he told me that the next many years were going to be "up and down." I was going through a difficult period due to some overlapping planetary movements in my astrological chart.

As a remedy, he gave me a list of things to do. He gave me a sun salutation to do every morning first thing. He told me to wear and eat yellow things every Thursday for two months and to wear a gold-encased yellow sapphire, which I promptly ended up buying from him for additional funds. There was a certain prayer he had arranged on my behalf with some *sadhus* (holy men) he knew who lived by the Ganges at a certain set time and day. That, of course, was going to cost me additional money. He also told me to read the "Hanuman Chalisa" (a prayer sung to Lord Hanuman, the monkey God) every day, at any time. He also gave me a mantra that I had to repeat 108 times per day while looking at a photo of Sarasvati, the Hindu goddess of knowledge and wisdom. He said that if I did all the things he recommended, there was 99.9 percent chance that my marriage would be saved and everything would be good for the rest of my life. In the 0.1 percent chance that the marriage was not saved, everything would wrap up very fast in the languishing open divorce proceedings at hand.

Well, I certainly and diligently did all that he asked me to do, and for as long as he said I needed to. Still, I was not able to save the marriage, and the wrapping up process of the divorce was still about nine months away. It was what it was: a desperate man trying what he must. I am sure at some level all this exercise and motion of doing something, anything, did act like a balm to temporarily distract and heal me. As I look back at this time in my life nine plus years ago, I am glad I went through the experience. To me, life is all about learning, growing, and moving through our experiences no matter how hard they are.

By this time, I had started reading some of the great ancient Hindu wisdom of *The Upanishads* and the *Bhagavad Gita.* I gravitated to all these texts first because of my familiarity growing up with them in India; I had heard their names from my father and some of our relatives. Everyone reminded me that these books were something I must read at some point soon. Well, it sounded like my time had come to try and read them. I did, and while I agreed with what was said, I couldn't process it at much more than a very shallow intellectual level.

One morning I was sipping tea, sitting with my dad outside on the veranda upstairs at our house in Sonipat, and I came upon a section in one of the local newspapers, describing different kinds of karma based on Hindu philosophy. I remembered one of my dad's friends telling me that what I was going through was because of my karma. What was this thing called karma?

There was the *Prarabdha* karma, or matured karma, the karma of our past actions that has matured and needs to be born in the current life. It was compared to an arrow that has already left the bow of an archer. Maybe what I was going through with my divorce was part of my Prarabdha karma, the result of a prior entanglement with my wife in a previous life. All we can do with this one is to bear it and make sure we don't generate new karma in the process, called *Agami*, or forthcoming, karma based on our present responses when bearing Prarabdha. It seemed like the unfolding of my life events were almost out of my hands, based on ancient Hindu sages, as that was mostly my Prarabdha, but my actions, reactions, and responses to the unfolding Prarabdha is where my psychological free will really lay.

If my daily responses to my unfolding life events were bad or hurtful or negative toward people, all I was doing was generating new Agami karma that would then get added to my already accumulated karma, called *Sanchita* karma, from all my lives lived so far. Sanchita was compared to all the arrows in the quiver.

So what I gathered from that article was that I had full control over my actions in my present life, and those actions ultimately would determine my destiny or future lives, so to say, and that I was always in charge of my journey via my daily actions. Made sense. From a Hindu perspective then, a predetermined life simply meant that I, because of my Agami karma in response to the unfolding Prarabdha over which I had no control in each life, in a sense continue to create my own web of cause and effect (karma) that I stay caught in each time. Only I could change my destiny with right thoughts and thus right actions in the here and now to try and break this cycle. This way, I could stop creating new negative karma and, in fact, start creating merit (i.e., good karma) as I went along to offset and try to burn off some of my Sanchita, the remaining arrows in the quiver. I also read in that article that meditations and practicing mindful awareness in our daily living can also help burn off some of our Sanchita karma. I took good notes from that article.

By the time October rolled around in 2006, I knew in spite of all my efforts and those of the greater God's through Mr. Sharma's intervention, this marriage of mine was not going be saved. We had put our house on the market that summer already, and it was a tough housing market by then, especially for larger properties, even in Tiburon.

When we are in the midst of intense pain and suffering, we become almost numb to it. That was my case by the end of 2006. I was completely extended on all fronts—expectations of my family in India to take care of my ailing father, running the hedge fund I was soon to close, dealing with my lawyer, and taking care of my kids. The extent of my mental trauma became evident to me when, in December 2006, I ended up going to a doctor for a prescription of Viagra because my whole system had practically shut down by then. I didn't like the feeling of taking Viagra, so I remember using them only a couple of times. This is how much stress my system was under in hindsight.

What saved me as I look back at those times is the fact that I didn't run away and hide in alcohol or drugs of any kind to avoid my pain. I slowly but surely ended up dissolving my pain and frustrations. It took a while though. Bearing and not running away from all this intense pain also served to make my eventual flowering that much more sweet and intense on the upside. Pain and joy, I realized then, were simply two sides of the same coin.

By April 2007, our divorce was finally settled. I felt more settled emotionally as well. Our kids were doing fine. I realized that our children, just like all children, simply wanted to be loved, accepted, and appreciated by their parents, be it in one or two homes. I remember my younger son, Arkin, mentioning that he felt so much luckier that he had two homes to live in like so many of his other friends. So cool, I thought.

As I write and get to reflect on those times nine plus years ago, it is so easy to see that it was all meant to be, all part of a bigger drama and plan to force me to crack open from within. That was the real purpose of all my intense pain and suffering.

I had gained about ten pounds going through my ordeal and ended up joining the Bay Club in Marin. I also realized that mere physical exercises and going to the gym to work out would not permanently lower my psychological temperature and how I felt within. I used to work out and would feel better as some of my frustration and aggression within would dissipate, only to reappear again.

I knew then that my anger was arising from my way of thinking, and I had to understand and shift this thinking. And this shifting in my thinking wouldn't happen just by going to the gym longer and working harder. I had to develop a meditation practice to be able to dissolve some of my accumulated anger and frustration. I also had to stop pointing my finger at other people as the source of my problems and start looking within myself to see what needed to change so I could shift my thinking from deep within.

I decided to try yoga and took some classes at various local yoga studios and settled on Iyengar yoga. I really liked Iyengar yoga and what it did for my body and mind. Soon I was getting pretty good at many of the physical postures. Yoga definitely helped me get more centered within.

By early December 2007, our Tiburon house sold, and I decided to live in Belvedere on the water for the next couple of years. I quickly found and rented a house, threw all my stuff in it, and got on a plane to go be with my family since my father was now on his deathbed.

During 2007 alone, I had visited India three times, this being the last, mostly to take care of my dad, to take him to different psychiatrists in Delhi, Rohtak, and other towns close to where he lived in Sonipat. The biggest challenge with dealing with depression, I was learning, was that since it is an ailment you can't see, the medication is mostly trial and error to see what could eventually work. That required patience and real-time feedback between the patient and the doctor. This was proving to be very challenging in our case, as my father was getting worse. It was getting really hard for everyone in the family to try to figure out what was working or not for him. He had almost stopped eating. We often had to force feed him. He was a skeleton of a man. Only two years before, he was like a horse, healthy and fit. It was very hard for me to see him become a vegetable like this. I wondered what kind of Prarabdha karma he was going through and why.

Here was a man I had admired all my life for his honesty. As I reflect on those times, I can categorically say that I have so far never met a human being who was as honest to the core as my dad was. Bar none. He also helped so many people get jobs while he was working as a managing director of Hartron, a Haryana government-owned state electronics corporation in Chandigarh. Hartron, under my father's leadership from 1975 on, was responsible for laying the ground work and attracting electronics industries in Gurgaon. What Gurgaon is today, humming and buzzing with nonpolluting high-technology companies from all over the world, was the brainchild of my father and his team at Hartron.

In the process of granting land to many company executives, I remember so many times he had to literally accost would-be entrepreneurs from our house because instead of having good and worthy projects for getting allocations of this precious land, they would offer Hartron proposals of fictitious-sounding projects. They did this in the hopes of getting land that would, over time, greatly appreciate, as it has. They would also try to bribe my dad, and it was then that he had to ask them to leave the house, as he would get really upset at their gall. He was well-known to not accept bribes.

My dad was a big Gandhian. He loved the simplicity and high morals of Gandhi and clearly lived them all his life. In those last months, it was really hard for me to see this frail man whom I loved so dearly and deeply, not only because he was my father but also because he had been such a role model for me all my life.

I knew I had to try and understand, if I possibly could, why his life had taken such a harsh turn toward the end. Here was a man who had only helped people all his life and had lived such a happy, moral, and just life. Why was he being made to go through this? Clearly there was a larger force at work deciding our direction. I was later to learn fully that this larger force—the universal cause-effect phenomenon—is governed only by our own thoughts and resultant actions that continue to bind us in our own self-made web over lifetimes lived.

My father gave me plenty of freedom to express myself growing up. Among his three children, I was clearly his favorite. Growing up in Chandigarh, I remember accompanying him on many of his official trips to Delhi and traveling in his official white ambassador car with a red light on the top, reserved for VIPs. We would hang out together as he went about his day at work. We were best buddies, and he used to say we were to be best friends for the next one hundred years.

Sudeep Balain

It was so hard for me, toward the end of 2007, to see this man of so much strength and stature incapable of even taking care of his everyday needs. The family took care of him, and we did the best we could for him. I would look at him and wonder why he was being made to go through this when all he did was bring happiness and help to all he could. I would often ask him in those later months about karma, life after death, and so on. He was a hard-core scientist of physics, trained in the United States, very rational and left-brained and would dismiss outright any such conversation. He used to love the Vedas and had read the Rig Veda in Hindi many times as I recall. He very much disliked the idol worship that my mom used to indulge in, though he never stopped her.

As the new year of 2008 came, I flew back to Belvedere to be with my kids, leaving my dad hanging by not much more than a thread. I knew in my heart that he could go any time and that I had done the best I could for him, as had everyone else in the family. His karma was taking him where it must. The Prarabdha must be borne. My mother, being wise, was sad but not overly emotional and did what she could for him till the end. My sister-in-law, Kitab, and my older brother, Anand, did most of the day-to-day work and upkeep to keep him going till the end. When I left for home this time, I brought with me a photo of him when he was much younger that I used to like a lot and got it framed.

Part Three: Finding Firmer Ground—Belvedere

Years of 2008 and 2009

CHAPTER 1

Four Types of Yoga and Their Purpose

Y OGA MEANS UNION with our higher self within. It is our process of becoming whole. There are four ways suggested in Hindu philosophy for transcending our ego to achieve this union within—karma and Bhakti, Jnana, and Raja yoga. Depending on one's temperament, one can choose whichever path comes naturally. If done properly with patience and discipline, the ego gets transcended, and this union within with what is called *Atman* results in a state of Samadhi or lasting ecstatic bliss. There is then a complete transformation of the person. One is said to become free, self-realized, or enlightened, the sole purpose of our earth incarnations.

As an aside I want to mention here that the real purpose of doing the asanas, or physical yoga work-out postures that we primarily do in the West, is supposed to simply be a preliminary step to get the body centered and ready for the much-deeper and bigger work of self-realization within that I mention above. In the West we tend to focus primarily on the physical exercise part of yoga and think that is all yoga is.

Even in the *Yoga Sutras of Patanjali*, which I discuss in more detail later in the book, doing asanas is only one of the eight limbs of his Astanga yoga as discussed in his second book, the *Sadhana Pada.* Patanjali's primary focus throughout the first two books of his *Yoga Sutras*, the *Samadhi* and *Sadhana Padas*, is the yogi's self-work to make his mind one-pointed, to reduce the *kleshas* or distractions and afflictions of his mind. The more this is done, the closer Samadhi gets to be at hand for the yogi. The whole process of self-realization is that simple.

Another clarity I wanted to highlight here that a lot of people miss is the fact that when Patanjali mentions asana in his Astanga yoga work, asana is a Sanskrit word meaning "sitting" posture, not the physical Hatha yoga we do in the West. He wanted the yogi to sit firm and comfortable so as to be able to focus (again) on removing the afflictions of his mind. That is the primary work, not the physical movements of the body. All the yogi's efforts per Patanjali are supposed to be focused on the mind and its distractions and how to make the mind "gather in one place," devoid of all its distractions. That state is the state of our Samadhi per Patanjali. Samadhi in Sanskrit means to gather everything together in one place.

So the basic purpose of doing any of the four mentioned yogas in this chapter is to self-purify, to clean ourselves within so as to achieve this oneness with our higher self, and the attribute of this higher self is unconditional love. This is when we achieve Samadhi, and the seer (Atman) and seen (our ego-driven phenomenal world perceived through our senses) become one.

Examples of karma yogis in our recent history would be great beings of light, like Mother Teresa of Calcutta, Gandhi, and Martin Luther King, among others who selflessly worked to take care of, heal, and free the people around them. The key phrase is *selfless work*. Doing selfless work without expectation of any fruits of our work. That is karma yoga.

Bhakti yogis would be sages like Kabir, the Sufi mystics who were always connected and drunk with the love of God within, Ramakrishna, and Meera and her love for Krishna. Bhakti yogis primarily indulge in devoted prayer and worship to get past their personal sense of identity or ego. In Christian faith Bhakti yogis would be great enlightened beings of light like Saint Francis of Assisi and Saint Teresa of Avila. In fact, in my mind, the ascent of the soul in four stages that Saint Teresa discusses of her own mystic experiences is none other than her process of self-realization, the union she experienced with God within and without.

A good example of a Jnana yogi would be the great sage Ramana Maharshi from Tamil Nadu state in the South of India and the spiritual teacher Jiddu Krishnamurti of Ojai, California. A Jnana gets to understand and thus transcend the ego personality by engaging in self-inquiry via self-awareness. Layer by layer, the yogi gets to reject who or what he or she is not through the process of *neti neti* (not this not this) to get to the full awareness of the divinity within (Atman) that we always were and are. You are that, as Ramana would often tell his devotees. Simply remove your ignorance (transcend your ego) to realize that.

Raja yoga is the process of dissolving or transcending our ego primarily through a meditation practice. Yogananda of Self-Realization Fellowship (SRF) immediately comes to mind as a prime recent example of such a great enlightened yogi of our times.

On our work of flowering or liberation, we can and should use all of these yoga paths simultaneously. That is what I did to intensify my work and resultant flowering. I could be involved in selfless work via my church or synagogue, doing daily meditations, devoted prayers and worship, all the while engaged in self-inquiry to deepen my spiritual knowing every day.

Indian yoga philosophy suggests that the main reason for our continued bouts with unhappiness, anxiety, and fear largely stems from our lack of connection within with our higher selves. This higher self can be called Soul, Holy Spirit, Atman, Love, Truth, or God. So if we are able to transcend whatever comes between us and our higher self within—our ego or our ignorance—we immediately become a buddha (one who is awake) or a self-realized being.

You Are Love

As I progressed along on my own spiritual flowering, I came to fully understand and appreciate that we as human beings are responsible for our present state of affairs. Often people think that because Hindus believe in reincarnation, it simply implies we not make any effort toward our self-improvement and keep bearing our karma, wherever we find ourselves in our lives. Not so at all. It is actually the opposite. As I said earlier when detailing the different kinds of karma, we as human beings are fully and completely responsible through our everyday actions for the trajectory of our current and future lives. This we get to do each day as we express our thoughts and actions in our everyday relationship encounters.

How should we define what our ego or ignorance is?

To me my ego is my identity, my personality, who Sudeep is today because of all my past conditioning, my experiences so far, my unfulfilled desires, my beliefs, my dogmas—all this and more that makes me live in my own prison of ideas and thoughts, the colored lens through which I perceive the world moment to moment, which then forms my incoming reality. I then lose sight of the innate knowledge and fact that I am perfection to start with, a piece of the divine Source itself. All our work of self-transformation is simply to remove this ignorance of ours that we tend to associate so intimately with.

Clearly, every person's lens is colored ever so differently. This is due to our childhood, our household religion or family traditions, and our beliefs or ways of looking at life—a Hindu might also suggest here that it's due to one's *samskaras,* or tendencies and inclinations, one brings from previous lives. Why are some people more prone to abusing drugs or alcohol than others? Such tendencies continue to migrate with us till they are fully understood and dissolved via our efforts of self-awareness and inquiry, which we will be discussing soon. In my mind, the good work of regression therapists on their patients so they can lose weight or quit smoking or drinking or any other such habit is also often based on this same premise of bringing our habits with us from previous lives. Such tendencies and habits are stored deep in our psyches or unconscious minds and get released when we are in a deep state of relaxation. Whatever is not understood and thus fully dissolved in this life at death, we get to take with us to be untangled later.

What does transcending our ego or removing our ignorance mean?

To me it means a state of equanimous mind that has stepped back from itself to simply watch its own activities, unhindered. It is the same state as having an empty mind.

We cannot have a state of mind devoid of all thoughts. But we can definitely have a state of mind with fewer thoughts coursing in it. I noticed that as the nature of each thought is fully understood by me, its hold on my mind lessens and eventually dissipates. Often then, such thoughts simply stop showing up or course around in my

You Are Love

mind without causing me to take any action or notice. My mind then innately, naturally, starts becoming more restful, peaceful, and quiet. This way, as I kept understanding myself (my thoughts) more in full self-awareness, I also kept releasing myself (my ego) more. My ego is merely my accumulated thoughts.

This to me is transcending my ego. We then get to get out of our own way. Then my mind does what it has to do to fulfill its daily activities, and I, as a watcher or seer, simply watch and see the unfolding drama without personal conflict.

And finally, how do we experience this state of transcendence?

I experience this state when I am able to live and function fully and completely in my responsibilities toward my family, friends, and myself while partaking fully of this world with detachment. Detachment is the key requirement here. Without detachment, transcendence of the ego doesn't show up. Detachment does not mean indifference. Detachment truly comes about when we are content within. Only when we are content within through our full understanding are we able to let go and release (i.e., become detached from anything, including ourselves, our egos). It is a very high spiritual station.

Detachment is a deep state of being and living from the heart with compassion for all that also shows up when we are equanimous. When we are detached from all, we truly care for all. Equanimity and detachment go hand in hand. And from these two arises unconditional love that wells up within us automatically. This love is nonpossessive, choiceless, and equal toward one and all. This love is the highest spiritual station.

The more we transcend our egos, the more we get to taste this love within as perpetual bliss and ecstasy. There is a direct relationship here. As you can tell, the whole thing is a circular loop. As one state is achieved, it almost pulls the other two ever closer toward itself within. Essentially, in my own direct experience, these three—detachment, equanimity, and unconditional love—become a loop that feed on each other and intensify, fully liberating us in the process.

Then one becomes like a lotus flower blooming in the mud and gunk—the push and pull of daily living—without being affected or touched by it. It sounds easy but is focused, hard work. The easiest way I found was to get a hold of any one of these three—love, detachment, or equanimity—within by reducing my ignorance or ego, by reducing the distance between the seer and what he sees.

I also realized as I went along on my journey that the first important state of mind I had to behold and maintain was equanimity. If I could not maintain daily equanimity, I could not build on my work. Detachment came next and then finally love within and without.

The more one can live in such a manner, the closer we are to our self-realization, our freedom—the basic reason for coming here on earth, our school.

CHAPTER 2

—◡—

Finding Yogananda and
Autobiography of a Yogi

DURING THE SECOND half of 2007, I remember going often to the local Barnes and Noble in the Corte Madera mall. I would spend plenty of time going through different genres of spiritual books to find answers to my general state of agitated beingness then. I remember picking up and passing over a book about some yogi with long hair from India once.

This day of March 13, 2008, I am again in the same area browsing through different books, and my eye goes back to the same book with the same Indian yogi with long hair as the cover of this book. He seems to be patiently looking at me. The cover of the book says over one million copies sold. I wonder why I have never heard of this dude. I pick up the book, start browsing through the various photos in the book, and decide to buy it. Along with that, I also end up buying a bunch more SRF (Self-Realization Fellowship) books for a total of seventy dollars.

Two days later, it is early afternoon, and I get a missed call from India. I see that the number is from my parents' house in Sonipat. I call back to find out from Kitab, my sister-in-law, that Dad passed away couple of hours prior. I was expecting this news. I tell her I will call her back once I have my flights figured out. I am calm and almost relieved thinking that Dad got to leave his depressed and weak body. Why keep suffering? I knew he would continue to live in higher realms, and I would always be with him here and in the hereafter.

As my luck would have it, I could not get a flight out of San Francisco till the next day. I called home and told them to not wait and to go ahead with the cremation right away as Hindu custom would demand. In a way I was re-lieved that I would not have to see his dead body. This way he would continue to live in my memories as I remem-bered him last.

I also got to reflect on the fact a bit later on the flight back from India that my discovering Yogananda two days before my dad's death was almost like my dad opening a new door for me and leaving me in good care before departing.

I immediately went to our village first and met my cousins and their families, as well as my dad's only re-maining younger brother, Zile Singh; his dear wife, Leela; and my nieces, Rupika and Anupama who were still there visiting from out of town. From there the males of the house walked to the village cremation grounds a bit outside Mehlana. It is still custom for the women of the house not go to the cremation grounds.

His pyre was still a bit warm. As custom has it, we looked for any remaining bones and found a couple of small ones and dug a hole and buried them. Here was such a great guy who achieved so much in his life, and all that was physically left of him would fit in a couple of buckets. The sight was humbling to say the least. Nature eventually gets to reduce man—doesn't matter who or how rich or how accomplished—to nothing. I wondered why we human beings have such large and insatiable egos when we are alive. Don't we know this end will come to each of us?

I stayed back for another thirteen days, which is also customary in Hindu faith. At the end of the thirteen-day mourning period, we had a big get-together where a large feast was organized to be shared among family and my dad's friends and well-wishers. My mom and the rest of the family were holding up really well. We all knew in our hearts we did the best we could for him. I took the next flight home to be with my kids and to start settling in my new place in Belvedere.

On getting back, I also immersed myself in the *Autobiography of a Yogi*. It took me a bit over three months, and I finished reading it on June 16, 2008. As is my habit, after finishing each book, I usually write on the front inside page some small one-line comments, like "Loved the book," "Must read," and so on so I will know next time I pick it up what I thought the time before. Also, if one of my kids decides to read them, the notes will help them figure out which books not to miss on their journey and unfolding.

Here are the comments I wrote on June 8, 2008, as I was close to finishing the book: "Time and again I have come back to the teachings of Yogananda and the *Gita* (*Bhagavad Gita*) as a thirsty man goes to the well of infinite wisdom. They clearly are the two best friends one can have or need."

I also went on the self-realization website, found out about the teachings of Yogananda (that would be mailed to me on a weekly basis) and signed up for them as well. As I look back, those periodically mailed teachings that started for me on July 16, 2008, and continued till December 10, 2009, were really beneficial in keeping me disciplined to stay on the path, which is harder starting out, and opening me up to the love within. I still have all those teachings in a binder. I also vividly remember the night. I was so excited I was driving to the SRF Temple on Ashton Street off Nineteenth Avenue in San Francisco. I had just found out there was a temple in the city. I went there many times in the evenings to sit and meditate in the small meditation hall upstairs.

I also got to know about Yogananda's guru, Yukteswar, who was also called the lion of Bengal (state in the Eastern part of India in which Calcutta and surroundings area fall) because of his high spiritual stature. On rereading the book recently, I realized there were many concepts and stories I didn't fully understand when I read the autobiography for the first time. Like the chapter on the materialization or resurrection of Sri Yukteswar and his descriptions of our etheric and causal bodies or the existence of heavenly mansions in the spirit world that Babaji (Lahiri's guru) manifested to fulfill a wish of his disciple Lahiri Mahasaya (Yukteswar's guru). I got to fully understand the reality and significance of both these stories and chapters in the book much later. With time, as I read more, I expanded my spiritual awareness via my meditations and by understanding more about the spirit world, which I will discuss in later chapters in the book, I fully got to appreciate why Yogananda shared these beautiful stories with his readers. The *Autobiography of a Yogi* is considered a spiritual classic of recent times and has sold well over four million copies.

As a general comment and observation, what I found really interesting on my rereading the autobiography recently is that what has been discussed by accomplished mediums and healers, like Ena Twigg and Betty Shine (both of whom I will discuss later in the book) whom I have read about much more recently and what Yogananda discusses in his autobiography first written in 1946, are similar psychic experiences and physical materializations. Alec Harris, another British medium who had the special gift of physical materializations, during his séances, facilitated physical materializations of discarnate beings who on touching and hugging by his audience felt and looked as we living humans do. Yogananda mentions a couple of times in his chapter on the resurrection of his guru Yukteswar how hard he was holding on to his guru who to him felt completely human and normal.

Yogananda also discusses his psychic abilities of clairvoyance, telepathic connection, and mediumship while growing up. Quantum mechanics, as we know in the last forty-plus years, has been repeatedly proving the validity of nonlocal communication via lab-like experiments. All these similarities of such paranormal experiences over time and place and the emerging validity via science of such experiences have been really reassuring for me. Newtonian science as we know it today is only three hundred-plus years old, while humanity has been walking this earth for thousands and thousands of years more. I have no doubt that over time science will also be able to prove how the phenomenon of John of God healings take place, which have been going on for over fifty years now in Brazil, and the enigma of Ze Arigo, who was able to perform over two hundred surgeries per day with his rusty knife with no infections or pain, will also be understood. I will discuss both of these phenomena in greater detail later in the book.

It all ties together—that is my basic message—as long as one is able to stay curious and keep an open mind along the way.

By now I had also signed up for the SRF world convocation held each year in the first week of August in Los Angeles. What an amazing experience that was to be for me.

I arrived the night before and was staying at the hotel where the convocation was being held. Downstairs there was a movie showing on the life of Yogananda. I quietly sat in one of the front-row seats. The first thing that struck me when I saw Yogananda in the movie and on the large portrait on a pedestal on the side of the stage where the movie was being shown was the complete unconditional love emanating from his eyes, his whole being. I had tears in my eyes. I knew I was home. I just sat there and watched the movie and the various famous personalities, like Ravi Shankar, George Harrison, and many others, talk about how their lives were transformed once they came into contact with either SRF or Yogananda personally or after reading his autobiography.

Over the next many days, I sat in one of two big halls at the hotel that seated I believe over five thousand people. There were white people, brown people, black people, and every color in between. There was just love, excitement, and acceptance everywhere. I just stayed open and kept taking it in.

I loved sitting in the daily *kirtans* (devotional singing) and some of the talks given by various senior SRF brothers. The one-hour meditation sittings were difficult frankly, but I did what I could.

I think it was that year, in 2008, that Brother Anandamoy gave a fascinating talk on the wisdom of the *Gita* with amazing clarity. I remember being so impressed and moved that I went over to talk to him later that day in the large outside patio area under the Indian-looking tent where he was milling around with everyone. I thanked him profusely and dutifully went to the bookshop and bought all his available DVDs, two of which are listed in the DVD list toward the end of this book. Over the years, I have come to realize that the experience of clarity of essential truth is pretty rare, even among advanced spiritual people.

Fast-forward to about a year ago, in 2014, when the movie *Awake: The Life of Yogananda* (also mentioned as a must-see in the DVD list at the back) came out in theaters in the United States. I saw the movie four times at the Smith Rafael Theater and told everyone I knew or didn't know to go see it. All we can do is do our bit of trying to help others on the path; what people do with it is their karma and journey. I feel happy and complete just having done my bit.

As part of the convocation that year, I signed up for three bus tours, to the Mother Center, to Hollywood Temple, and to his crypt site at Forest-Lake Memorial Park. On successive trips to the convocation in 2009 and 2010 (with my oldest son, Rohan), I also ended up going to the Encinitas Temple and Retreat and the amazing temple and retreat setting at Lake Shrine. One has to simply visit to experience the love and joy among each flower and each tree at these locations and, of course, within each of the brothers and sisters of the SRF organization.

From that first visit, I brought back individual photos of Yogananda and Yukteswar, and the SRF travel altar, which has the six great yogis pictured—Jesus, Sri Krishna, Yogananda, Yukteswar, Lahiri Mahasaya, and Baba ji. I had all of them framed in the best wood possible. Thus started my altar at home. I started sitting in daily meditations, often difficult initially, but I kept going as Yogananda would have wanted.

I also remember taking photos of Yogananda, Yukteswar, and the SRF travel altar that I also bought from that first LA convocation trip for my parents' Sonipat house shrine. On one of my trips that year to India, I got them framed, and they are still there in our home shrine. It is so cool to see the SRF yogis sitting alongside photos of Laxmi, Shiva, Kali, Durga, and Ganesh. They are all one. Indeed so.

I was to come back two more times—for the annual Los Angeles world convocation in 2009 and with my oldest son, Rohan, whom I had made an SRF member by then, in 2010. He was twelve. For his first visit, Rohan did really well. He sat in some meditations and attended some kid-focused spiritual talks, and the rest of the time, he simply skated out in the big patio area upstairs in the hotel. We used to deposit his skateboard at the back of the big convention hall as we would enter, where the big cameras were set up.

I also remember that in 2008, on my trip to India after I visited the annual LA world convocation, I had ordered online, via the SRF website, two Hindi translations of the autobiography book since my sister-in-law in Sonipat couldn't read English. So these two books were shipped from YSS (the SRF arm in India) to the United States, and then I took them back to India—one copy each for my sister's home in Delhi and for my sister-in-law's home in Sonipat. This still sounded more efficient than trying to order them in India directly through YSS and then relying on the local Indian mail to get them.

I will end this section by mentioning my experience the first time in 2008 when our bus snaked its way up the hill to the entrance of the Mother Center and we disembarked by the big open gates. As we all walked onto the grounds, on each side all the brothers were standing and smiling with folded hands to welcome us and the sisters. I remember some in beautiful yellow saris (traditional Indian wear for women) smiling and simply welcoming us. I was overwhelmed with the unconditional love. To me this was Yogananda's legacy at its best, vibrant and fully alive. It was almost as if the master was waiting for all of us upstairs in his room. I couldn't control the tears in my eyes. I had never experienced this much unconditional love before. I continued to support the SRF organization during those years.

CHAPTER 3

Rotaplast Nagamangala Humanitarian Mission

ROTAPLAST CAME FROM rotary and plastic surgery. I remember during May 2008 going to the rotary meeting in downtown Belvedere at the local chapter there. Someone talked about the upcoming Rotaplast trip to a small town in South India called Nagamangala, a couple of hours from Bangalore, to do cleft-lip and -palate surgeries on poor kids in India. Such trips around the world had been going on for Rotaplast for many years. Each trip cost over $75,000 if I recall, where a US-based team of three to four plastic surgeons and as many as seventeen to twenty nurses, orthodontists, pediatricians, and anesthesiologists would volunteer their precious time and effort to do one hundred-plus operations on kids mostly living in rural and poor areas around the world. The team was still looking for a few more volunteers who would have to pay their own airfare. I loved the idea and signed up immediately. I had been to Bangalore during the summer of 1983 for a training at Bharat Electronics Limited when I was still attending my engineering school on the outskirts of town and had liked that whole area. I mainly loved the idea of helping these prospective kids and their families who would never be able to afford this kind of surgery at local hospitals, even in India. Growing up in India, I knew how expensive any kind of surgery like this would be.

I remember we landed at Bangalore airport at around three in the morning local time, weary from the long flight from San Francisco, and upon coming out of the airport, we were greeted with these beautiful, heavy garlands of local flowers—the scent of them I still can smell. We were welcomed with such acceptance and appreciation by the local rotary-chapter members. We squeezed into a small bus and were quickly on our way on dusty Indian roads for our three-hour bus ride to the local medical-college dorm, where we were crowded in three per room. I remember the bathroom mirror was so small and hazy that you could barely make out your face outline while shaving. We did have hot water, so we were in business.

I and another local Joe, also ex-Wall Street, were given the major task of autoclaving all surgical instruments. We were given major training once we got there on how to best handle the instruments, how long to keep them in the autoclave oven, and other such important details. It was a tough job. There were days we would start around six in the morning and go straight till six or seven in the evening with a short break for lunch. There were some adult severe-burn victims who also came for help. Though this was not the charter of the trip, the plastic surgeons would never say no, knowing full well that for such patients this would be their only hope and opportunity.

This was also the first time I had seen a human body opened up. I remember wondering then that if the skin is only a few millimeters deep and since we all looked the same within, why was there still so much hatred and discrimination based on our skin color? Why didn't people realize and see it this way?

We had so much fun. On the weekend, we ended up going sightseeing to some local South Indian temples. I also remember some of us got pretty tired of eating the same kind of foods for breakfast, lunch, and dinner by the time the second week rolled around. I, being Indian and thus supposedly local, ventured out and found a local restaurant some distance from our dorms that had chips, coke, beer, vegetable burgers, and chocolate bars. Man, we were excited. That evening all thirty-plus of us, as a group, set out and emptied the place of all food and drink. I think we went again once but gave the restaurant a heads-up that we were coming.

Joe and I would often go for evening walks into the fields close by the medical college where we were staying. Indian-village living has always drawn me in. The simple and almost innocent ways of the villagers have a special place in my heart because I was also born in a village. One day we ended up walking far and came upon a small temple in a field. The local Hindu temple seemed to be closed. Joe and I made our way in, and soon the priest came by, blessed us, and put a red mark on Joe's forehead. I remember Joe being very excited being blessed at the local temple.

On the last few days of the trip, we were appreciated so much by the whole local community, as the kids by then had healed and had their stitches removed and looked normal for the first time. The look of love and appreciation in the faces of the parents was so touching and made the whole trip worthwhile. Somehow the more loving and selfless work we engage in, the more love and joy we feel in our own heart as well. Science via quantum mechanics was also validating that we are all connected nonlocally by consciousness or love or whatever name one wants to give this medium, but I and others on the team knew this from our heart.

As a life coach today, I tell my clients to do as much volunteer work as needed to find that love connection within that is patiently waiting to be discovered in each of us. One of the best ways to heal ourselves is to give of our time and energy selflessly to those we deem strangers. No one is a stranger; we are all connected at the root level as human beings, but to experience this connection live, and to open us up, we need to do this kind of work as much as needed. This I learned firsthand on that trip.

To thank the whole team for our time and effort, there was a major celebration one evening filled with drama, dance, and food. Each of us was called to the stage, with hundreds of the medical-college and local-community participants in the audience, and was given a certificate of appreciation and a customary Indian shawl (light blanket).

I recall supporting Rotaplast during that time and remember going to their fundraisers at their center in San Francisco. It is a really wonderful organization to get involved in.

I remember also organizing a slide show at my kids' school, Marin Montessori School in Corte Madera, where all the kids in the school squeezed into one large classroom to watch Angelo (one of the founders of Rotaplast), Joe, and I give a presentation on all that we did and covered on that trip. The kids thought it was really cool.

CHAPTER 4

Eknath Easwaran

I FIRST HEARD Eknath's name from a yoga teacher whose class I was taking at Yoga Works in Corte Madera. One day in class, she mentioned that the best translation she had read of the *Bhagavad Gita* was the one done by Eknath. I came home, researched the book on Amazon, checked out the reviews, and ended up buying the three books in that series offered by the Blue Mountain Center of Meditation (BMCM), the spiritual center that Eknath founded and left behind for his dear wife, Christine, to run and grow.

I read all three in the series—the *Bhagavad Gita*, *The Upanishads*, and the Dhammapada. In the years following, I also read the translations done by Juan Mascaro of these three books and the translation of the *Gita* done by Swami Prabhavananda of the Vedanta Society, Hollywood. These have been the most astute and beautiful translations I have read so far.

In my opinion, in the main, the *Gita* is urging each of us to do the spiritual hard work of transcending our egos and reducing our ignorance by increasing our self-awareness about how we act in our daily relationships and how we treat ourselves and others. In my experience we end up treating others as we look at, perceive, and treat ourselves first within. We are all projecting from the inside out. If I am harsh and critical of myself, I will simply end up projecting that harshness toward people I interact with on a daily basis. So by simply and honestly watching ourselves in our daily actions, we can start to dissolve and keep loosening the intensity of our deep-seated emotions, like anger, hate, jealousy, envy, and so forth that most of us carry around and keep reliving on a daily basis. The key is to stop giving them new fuel via our thoughts. For that, we have to simply become a choiceless observer of our thoughts. Unless we detach from our deep-seated emotions and look at them, we will not be able to diminish their hold on us. This I can say categorically from my own direct experience and observations.

This is worth repeating here: without our choiceless observation, the intensity of such emotions within us and their hold on us will not diminish. Time often does not heal; it simply makes that particular painful event lie dormant to be inflamed again as the right circumstances show up, which they will. Our work then is to dissolve, via understanding and awareness, our mental and emotional baggage or defilements, our collective ignorance, that we keep carrying around from relationship to relationship. This is the basic fight that the *Gita* is calling us to make each day. This, to me, is the basic universal message of the *Gita* to humanity. *Gita* to me is not a Hindu text; it is a universal text. Sri Krishna in the *Gita* urges *Arjuna*, which is you and I, to boldly take up this much-needed task of self-realization at hand. Any work done on this path of ours in each life never goes to waste, Krishna reminds us.

Gandhi has been quoted as saying the following about the *Gita*:

The Gita is the universal mother. She turns away nobody. Her door is wide open to anyone who knocks. A true votary of Gita does not know what disappointment is. He ever dwells in perennial joy and peace that passeth understanding. But that peace and joy come not to skeptic or to him who is proud of his intellect or learning. It is reserved only for the humble in spirit who brings to her worship a fullness of faith and an undivided singleness of mind. There never was a man who worshipped her in that spirit and went disappointed. I find a solace in the Bhagavad Gita that I miss even in the Sermon on the Mount. When disappointment stares me in the face and all alone I see not one ray of light, I go back to the Bhagavad Gita. I find a verse here and a verse there, and I immediately begin to smile in the midst of overwhelming tragedies—and my life has been full of external tragedies—and if they have left no visible or indelible scar on me, I owe it all to the teaching of Bhagavad Gita.[1]

Gandhi was a rather small and thin vegetarian of barely one hundred pounds and was also perpetually on some kind of fast, especially during the last years before India's independence in 1947. He got all his inner strength and nourishment from the *Gita*. He used to have one of his devoted followers read passages from the *Gita* during his morning and evening prayers. Such is the inherent clarity and intensity of the *Gita's* message. Every time one reads it, a new door of depth seems to open up within.

The Upanishads (approximately 1200 BCE), which came long before the *Gita* (400 BCE), were written and complied by ancient yogis and rishis who, via their deep and long meditation practices, came to an understanding that *I am God*, or that there is a part of God (they called it Brahman) in me as well (called *Atman*) and that like the Brahman, the Atman is deathless. This Atman is like a watcher, a witness, a seer, within us, of our unfolding daily life drama. It can be compared to the movie screen on which the movie of our lives gets played without affecting the screen. Once the movie is finished (each incarnation), the screen is still there as intact as ever and gets used for another movie till we finally, via our self-realization, achieve freedom from this wheel of Samsara. This also implies that we are perfected beings to start with at our root level, unstained and unstainable.

Sudeep Balain

The 108 remaining Upanishads, from about 220 that were originally thought to have been written, are a continuing commentary on the nature of Brahman (God) and its direct and impersonal link with the Atman (soul, spark of God, Holy Spirit) within each of us. To realize Brahman, our work then simply is to become one with this Atman within us through our process of self-realization. Our required efforts are comprised of our meditations and our increased awareness of this inherent nondual nature of reality and by continuing to internally purify ourselves by dissolving our conditioning.

Unlike the Western religions, where there seems to be at least an intended dualism or separateness between man and God, there is no such division as per the great ancient yogis and their experiences in deep meditations about the nature of reality, or God within and without, in *The Upanishads*. God (Brahman) and I (Atman) are always connected and one. I am that. Only the ignorance that I am not in our everyday living created by our egos needs to be understood and dissolved. This then becomes our spiritual work in each life so that we can ultimately realize this inherent oneness with God within and become free.

Later *Advaita* (nondual) *Vedantic* (the period starting with the end of the Vedas) texts, of which *The Upanishads* is the first and most important contributor, were developed by many including Valmiki in the Vasistha's yoga and Adi Shankara, who consolidated the doctrine of *Advaita*

Vedanta and wrote, among other works, his two most important Advaita texts: *Viveka Chudamini* and *AtmaBodha*. Adi Shankara was a die-hard and true Jnana yogi who died at the young age of thirty-two.

German philosopher Schopenhauer was so impressed with *The Upanishads* that he called the texts "the production of the highest human wisdom." Erwin Schrodinger, considered one of the fathers of quantum physics, who won a noble prize in 1933 for his discovery of wave mechanics, was an ardent devotee of the great German philosopher Schopenhauer, who read and wrote extensively about this oneness (unity) or interconnectedness between Brahman and Atman. The Newtonian physics of the past three hundred-plus years' rests on the separateness and orderly movements of all matter in the universe. What if all matter is indeed not separate at the root level as the ancient yogis of India postulated in *The Upanishads*? What if some invisible fabric, like consciousness, is the medium that connects everything and everyone?

The Dhammapada is a collection of the sayings of the Buddha categorized around broad themes, like the nature of the mind, a flower, punishment, wisdom, and the like with the main purpose being the same as the previous two texts already discussed—to help us achieve self-realization. It is simply another avenue to take us within. Depending on one's temperament, one can choose among these three texts or, as in my case, study and practice all of them.

I visited Eknath's ashram many times, often to be on the beautiful grounds. I remember a smaller group of fifteen to twenty used to meet at a church closer to my house to discuss and penetrate deeper into concepts like the nature of our egos, self-will, and other teachings of Eknath. I continued to support BMCM for a couple of years till I was involved more intimately with them. I also remember signing up for Eknath's "Thought of the Day" e-mail that, in those early years, proved to be very helpful to me in staying the course by being centered and reminded all day.

As I have read these three sacred texts time and again over the past ten years, each time a new, deeper door of perception and self-understanding has opened. God as love is present in each of us equally. The more open-minded we are to listening to its voice, the more we hear it and the further drawn we become to its sweet intoxication.

The deeper and more empty our vessel becomes of ourselves, our egos, the more can be poured into it. Only an empty cup is useful.

CHAPTER 5

Committee on the
Shelterless, Petaluma

I DON'T QUITE recall how the connection with the Committee on Shelterless (COTS) came about toward the fall of 2008. I visited the center in Petaluma with my kids. We toured the facility, and I showed my kids how people lived at these facilities, including some families with kids. Once, around thanksgiving that year, I also attended their dinner for residents and local homeless people who had no place to live or food to eat. These experiences, along with being very humbling for me, again and again reinforced the central theme that we are all one irrespective of where we find ourselves in life—that we are all children of the same God.

Often, when I give some money to a homeless person, my kids ask me why I do it each time—so-and-so can get a job and looks healthy, so why give to this one but not that one? My answer is always the same: Who am I to judge who to give to and not give to? If I want to help, I should simply help without judgment. None of us knows in our very brief encounters with homeless people what's going on inside them.

I continued to visit and support COTS financially for some time.

CHAPTER 6

Mother Teresa of Calcutta
Center, San Francisco

I WAS IN the eleventh grade at DAV College, Chandigarh, reading in the local newspaper about Mother Teresa being awarded the Nobel Peace Prize. She was a Christian nun, based primarily in Calcutta, who had been helping the sick and dying in India for many years. I had never been to Calcutta, but her being a Christian and primarily taking care of Hindus and Muslims in India just showed me her sheer uninhibited love of humanity in the name of Jesus. I remember thinking what an amazing and selfless woman she was. Mother Teresa was a great example of a karma yogi, one who engages in selfless service.

I used to read items and stories of her mission of sisters in newspapers and magazines, picking up sick and dying strangers from the streets of Calcutta and elsewhere in India. This selfless giving of oneself in love for humanity and God I somehow understood and connected with deeply, even at that time.

This was the same selfless love of people and God that I was to later get attracted to in the Sufis, the Baal Shem Tov, Jesus, Gandhi, Ramana Maharshi, Yogananda, Ramakrishna, Sai Baba of Shirdi, and Ze Arigo, the healer who used to operate and heal the poor and sick before Joao de Deus (John of God) in Brazil with his rusty knife. He would complete about two hundred free operations in a typical day and then head to a government job that used to give him under fifty dollars a month. And then there was the story of Chico Xavier, an almost illiterate automatic writer in Brazil who downloaded from the spirit world over four hundred books in his lifetime, many of which still have not been translated into English because their concepts are too complicated for our current human way of thinking and being. Chico ended up donating all the royalties from his books, estimated at over fifty million copies sold as of 2010, I believe, to local spiritist centers all over Brazil.

When I first heard of Joao de Deus of Brazil toward the end of 2012, I went to visit with him simply because I wanted to see how this man had been performing these operations and healing people the world over for fifty-plus years. What is this energy that one feels in his current rooms, at his spiritual center in Brazil, when one sits in meditation? How can he heal with just this energy? Is this energy what we call God then? I was so curious.

I did not know then, in 1979, that about thirty years later, starting in 2009, such personalities would start to take over my life and interest completely.

You Are Love

On one of my many trips to India when my dad was not well, in 2007, I took the kids with me, and we visited Mother Teresa's Jeevan Jyoti Center for handicapped kids in New Delhi. There were housed, if I recall, over one hundred kids at that center, mostly aged anywhere from two to ten years old. I had already been there on my own on a previous trip in 2006. My hope, in exposing my kids to this at their early age, was to put a seed of compassion, love, and giving in them for their later years.

Toward the end of 2008, I also found that there was a Mother Teresa center in San Francisco, and on one of my visits, I found that they used to run a homeless soup kitchen at a local fire station by the AT&T Park most days of the week.

I planned the timing of my next trip on a weekend and in such a way as to first sit in their simple chapel for a quiet meditation and then help the sisters load all the prepared food in their van and drive to the fire station as a volunteer. It was a lot of fun. The sisters were singing Christian songs of Jesus and his love of humanity and our love for him, and we were all laughing and having a good time. They didn't seem to have a care in the world. Most of the sisters in that van were from India if I recall correctly. We got to the fire station, and there were already some people waiting outside. More came by the time we rolled up the big garage doors. There had to have been close to seventy-five homeless people who were seated and hungry for food. Once the sisters got their attention, one of the sisters read from the Bible for about twenty minutes while the hungry faces kept looking impatiently.

We cleaned up afterward, mopping the floors and wiping down the tables, table covers, plastic white chairs, and kitchen, and we put everything back in its respective storage area. I loved it. The next weekend, I brought my three children, and we repeated the same routine. We all went to the chapel first and prayed to Jesus and Mary, and this time I drove my car, and we followed the van to the fire station. In those years, around every April 24, my birthday, I used to take my kids there and give a donation and sit and pray in the chapel for a bit. It felt like the most normal thing for me to do. On one such trip on my birthday, the head sister, a South Indian I recall, gave me a photo of Mother Teresa, which I promptly got framed, and she became a part of my growing altar where I would sit and meditate often.

This was to be the start of my intense love for Jesus and many other Christian saints, notably St. Ignatius and St. Francis Xavier, and of course Prophet Solomon, the great king of the Jews. That love kept building as I read about them more, and they all became part of my altar in a big way once I visited the healer John of God in Brazil in 2013, on my first visit.

Jesus was already part of my altar when I started it in 2008 on coming back from my first of three annual SRF world-convocation visits. After 2013 I was to meet and commission a really good painter in San Francisco to paint a total of six oil paintings on wood, the smallest being a six-teen-by-thirty-inch of the Church of Dom Bosco in Brasilia, which I visited with a group of thirty Americans on my first trip to the Casa of John of God. These church altars kept getting bigger as I went along, with the last one being of the patron saint of Brazil, the dark-skinned virgin Mary of Aparecida, at thirty-by-forty inches with seven cherubs on both sides. I remember seeing a small framed photo of her in my friend's room at the Pousada Austria I was staying at in Abadiania during my second month-long visit to John of God. I borrowed it for a night, ended up keeping it for three, and knew that I had to get it painted. I remember I also bought a couple more rosaries on that trip.

What's with you and the Christian faith? Lots of my friends would ask this when they would come over. And then Solomon came into my life. I was not a Jew either as far as I knew. I would half seriously tell them that maybe I was a Christian and a Jew in one or many of my previous lives. When divine love comes, it simply washes over you; one has no control or decision-making power to choose where it comes from. As we go deeper, we come to un-derstand that the source is the same. The more I surren-dered, the more this love filled me up from within and without.

It is relatively easy for us to give to our church or tem-ple, to help our own supposed people. In hindsight, it was when I slowly started making that circle bigger and wider that the real inner connection with God and love deepened within me. We are all one—this understanding, first intellectually and later of living like so from my heart, truly played a very big role in leading me to the current state of perpetual happiness and bliss in my daily living. Unknowingly, it was helping transform me from deep within my core.

It is never how much we give but that we give of ourselves selflessly to one and all, of our love, money, or time to those who we think are strangers. No one is a stranger; we are all connected in unconditional love within. This realization continued to open me up as I went along. I simply stayed open and kept listening to my heart. Whichever door opened, I walked through with full faith and trust. And this love kept washing over me, gently healing me of all my grief, hurt, and pain. By staying open, I let the divine love keep purifying me. To fully heal within, we have to learn to give of ourselves unconditionally to others. Such efforts often break open the hard casing of our ego that surrounds our heart and thinking, and we are thus able to start going within to accelerate our spiritual journey. I felt happier, stronger, and more in love with myself and humanity as 2008 was ending.

It was in February 2009 (I had to call the DMV to make sure) that I was to change the nameplate of my metallic dark-blue convertible 911 Porsche from its generic plate to WERAL01 (we are all one). I was clearly shifting deeply within and felt the need to express it without.

C H A P T E R   7

Belvedere Meditation Circle

As THE NEW year of 2009 started, I was meeting and attracting similarly minded people at the Bay Club, the local health club I still go to. I and another friend Jonathan I met there started a weekly meditation meet at my house. Soon Christin, another friend from the gym, also joined, and we would be pretty much always present at each meet. We would meet in the evenings starting six, and one of us would read a passage from a book of our choice. We would discuss it a bit and then sit in meditation, for about twenty minutes, to music. After that, we would simply open up and talk about whatever came to our mind. We would have one small candle burning in the middle, on a slate table, and the whole room used to get dark by the time we would finish talking and discussing. I remember Christin would often say, "I feel like I have come home." Then another friend of ours, Monica, whom I had also met at the gym, joined us as well. Everyone, as I recall, really looked forward to coming each week. We were a small group of about four to six people who met like that for many months into 2009. All these meditations and like-minded communal interactions kept opening me up and healing me from within. We used to talk about Kundalini, Tolstoy, Yogananda, life, and love. It was a beautiful setup while it lasted. During that time, I realized I was hugging more. The more I was opening up from within, the more open I was becoming to hugging. I remember we all used to hug each other incoming and outgoing. It was a great feeling of connection and oneness.

Since Jonathan and I were both seekers of the same divine love within, we often would venture out together to Spirit Rock to watch Jai Uttal perform or listen to a spiritual talk, or to San Francisco to see Krishna Das in concert. Once, we both drove to San Ramon to see Amma at her ashram, who was visiting the United States on her annual summer tour. I also remember going together to the Open Secret bookstore in San Rafael to see a special Kali puja performed by visiting monks from the Ramakrishna center in Calcutta. I remember taking my kids with me. It got late in the evening, and they lost interest halfway through. I was staying open to whatever was showing up. Those were indeed fun times of learning and growth.

CHAPTER 8

Gandhi

I HAVE WATCHED the movie *Gandhi* at home so many times over the years, and each time I have tears in my eyes at the start where his dead body, at the back of a tractor bed almost buried in flowers and covered majestically in the Indian tricolor flag, is slowly making its way with hundreds of thousands of Indians or more quietly walking behind it, some even running to keep pace. Gandhi simply was a phenomenon. Not just an Indian phenomenon, but a human phenomenon.

Everything that Gandhi's life was about, what it ultimately amounted to, is right there in my mind at his funeral procession. They say that the weight and stature of a man and a life well lived is in how many people show up at his funeral. In recent times in my mind, there hasn't been a match for Mahatma ("great soul," from the Sanskrit words *mahā*: great and *ātman*: soul) Gandhi yet. Rare is it in human history that a being of light with this much strength has walked this earth. Einstein said of Gandhi, "Generations to come, it may well be, will scarce believe that such a man as this one ever in flesh and blood walked upon this Earth."

As I said earlier, I grew up with Gandhi around me, my father reading his books, himself living a life that Gandhi exemplified as one of honesty, morality, simplicity, and, of course, nonviolence. My dad loved the *Gita* as did Gandhi. Gandhi also was a great example of a karma yogi who through selfless service ended up transcending his ego to achieve self-realization within.

As I read more of Gandhi, I realized that in so many ways his life and his living was so much of what Jesus taught (and so few actually follow): "To love thy neighbor, the kingdom of God is within you, love your enemies, and turn the other cheek." The whole philosophy of nonviolent resistance is based on the premise of mutual respect and love for the other—including the aggressor in spite of his aggression. By staying nonviolent through the aggressor's aggression, one simply ends up being a mirror for such a person's onslaught. Every time I have been shown the mirror in such a nonaggressive way, I have never repeated the same aggression again. It is amazing how well and deep such a learning can be. This approach requires more tolerance and patience but is clearly more effective and permanent. Plus, as Gandhi is so famous for saying, "An eye for eye only ends up making the whole world blind."[1] There has to be a better way. Gandhi's way of nonviolence was this better way.

I know this methodology works as I now practice it in my daily living. Whenever I encounter pettiness or meanness or short-temperedness, I step back, don't react, and take the high road, knowing that my aggressor is also a human being just like me, just more ignorant still of his or her true divinity within. I remind myself I was like him or her at one point as well. What is holy in me is also holy in my aggressor. We are all children of the same God. It is so easy to walk away without reacting or wanting to inflict verbal or physical pain this way. And every time I have done so, that same aggressor has never been aggressive in the same way. If anything, he or she feels humbled at my unconditional compassion and kindness. That softens the person. In my direct experience, the only way to deal with, dissolve, and not allow a coming aggression to stick to you emotionally is by being loving and peaceful toward the aggressor. This was how Gandhi won India's independence, from the might of the British Empire. And this is the message of peace and love he has left for us.

On researching Gandhi more, I also learned that his philosophy of nonviolence was deeply influenced and strengthened when he read Leo Tolstoy's *The Kingdom of God is within You* while still in South Africa around 1909, when he was forty years old. He put his then evolving nonviolent philosophy and living in an ashram (which was also inspired by Tolstoy's own life and living) into practice in South Africa on a smaller scale because of the limited local Indian population. As he saw success there, he then deployed it on a much larger canvas in India beginning in 1914. Never had such a huge experiment of nonviolent resistance, unconditional love, and respect ever been attempted anywhere in the world.

I was also to learn how deeply Martin Luther King was influenced by Gandhi and his philosophy. Not only did he read about Gandhi and his experiments in South Africa and India in great detail, he also took a five-week trip, in early 1959, to India to actually see and learn firsthand how Indians lived and thought in free India. I thought that was remarkable of Dr. King.

Gandhi kept stressing the need for unity and religious tolerance among the Indian Hindu and Muslim populations. He openly shared the practice of how the priest at his family temple, while Gandhi was growing up, would alternatively read from the *Gita* and the Koran and that it did not matter what book was being read as long as God was being worshipped. Whenever violence broke out, he would fast till it stopped. He said, "The only devils running around are the ones in our hearts and that is where all the battles ought to be fought."[2] This is straight out of the *Gita*, his "lifelong spiritual reference book" as he used to call it.

Even after India's eventual independence in 1947, Gandhi was not happy because of how it came about with the formation of India and Pakistan, India being for Hindus and Pakistan for Muslims. Right before his death on January 30, 1948, he still wanted to go to Pakistan to be among his fellow Muslim brothers to show his support and solidarity with them. It was not meant to be, unfortunately. Gandhi loved humanity, not just Indians. For me this was and continues to be his final message and greatest legacy.

What I now see in Gandhi is his depth of oneness with what he called "Truth or God within." This God within was the source of all his strength and wisdom and provided him with his often much-needed self-nourishment in his continued struggle and resistance on behalf of his people and his country. As well known as Gandhi is in India, I had an impossible time finding an eight-by-ten-inch photo of him to get framed as an addition to my altar. I have, on my altar, all those great teachers who have continued to help me on my spiritual evolution and flowering. Gandhi had to be added to that altar. After much looking, my then girlfriend found one on the Internet. Thanks to her, Gandhi is part of my altar.

As I look at the current state of the Middle East, the ongoing unrest and violence, I wonder if this Gandhian experiment should again be tried in earnest as a way of eventual peace and harmony in that region. But the effort should start not at the top but from the bottom up by everyday people joining hands on both sides and saying enough is enough. How long can we go on demanding an eye for an eye and to what end when we know from history it doesn't work?

CHAPTER 9

Ramana Maharshi

I DISTINCTLY REMEMBER the day I discovered Ramana. I was again at the same local bookstore in the same spiritual-book section where I had discovered Yogananda. I was scanning book covers row by row, and as I moved to the next row, I saw this beautifully smiling face looking at me. As my brain registered the face looking at me, I could not take my eyes off this book-cover face. There was so much unconditional love in those eyes looking back at me. I leafed through the book, which talked pretty highly about the nature of self-inquiry as a way to go deeper within on our journey of self-realization. I was later to learn that Ramana was a Jnana yogi of the highest order.

At the age of sixteen, Ramana had what can be best described as a mystical experience where he came close to death and realized he was not his physical body. That he was immortal and that there was a part of him that survives death. He lost all interest in the mundane, left home, started living in the hills nearby and meditating in different temples, and generally lived in isolated self-absorption.

Finally, his mother tracked him down and showed up one day and pled with him to come back home.

His well-known response to his mother goes something like this: "The fate of the soul is determined in accordance with its Prarabdha karma (the results of my past actions encountered in the present life). What is not meant to happen will not happen, however much you wish it. What is meant to happen will happen, no matter what you do to prevent it. This is certain. Therefore, the best path is to remain silent."[1]

Something of this deeply spoke to my heart. I bought the book and went to a local sushi restaurant for a quick dinner and leafed through the book. I clearly must have been staring at the cover for a while because I remember my waitress asking me who this dude was. The next day, the first thing I did was search the Internet for a photo of him to get framed for my altar. I knew right away this teacher had much to teach me, and I was being called to learn at his feet.

A Jnana yogi transcends his or her ego by the process of *neti neti* (not this not this). I thus looked at each thing or person or relationship that seemed to be important to me and simply kept going deeper within myself by asking the question who am I? again and again. Am I my money, my house, my car, my bank balance, my this and that? Eventually, if we are doing an honest self-inquiry, we get to the empty space within of simple awareness or consciousness. We then realize

"I am (already) that," what I am looking for. Nothing new needs to be acquired to become whole and happy. I am pure perfection to start with. Only this ignorance (the ego) that I am not needs to be understood and thus transcended. Suddenly, I realized the transitory nature of all the stuff I was surrounding myself with, material or human. There is a lot of shedding I went through this way, step by step.

A man who has transcended his ego becomes detached and thus peaceful and happy. As Ramana famously said, "Reality (God) is simply the loss of the ego."[2] Again, as I mentioned earlier in the book, transcending the ego does not mean leaving our worldly life and sitting on a mountaintop in India far away from everybody and everything. Quite the contrary. To me it means being in the world but not of the world. Functioning fully in the world and participating in all the activities that bring us joy and happiness, just not being attached to them. If one or many of the things (or people) I have in my life today disappear tomorrow, can I simply stay equanimous? Yes, I will miss them for a while, but can such ripples on the surface of our mind's lake soon get absorbed back in the stillness of the lake? If so I have transcended my ego. And as we go along, we realize that the duration of the ripples can keep getting shorter and shorter—we have full control over that process.

Ramana further tries to clear our understanding by saying, "Destroy your ego by seeking its identity."[3] By simply understanding what our ego (ignorance) is, we get rid of it—we transcend it. He tells us further that in this way of our self-inquiry and eventual liberation, no other religious or spiritual practices, like mantra japa (repetition), praying, performing of rituals, doing pilgrimages, and reading scriptures, are necessary.

This path is indeed direct and simple in my own experience. What is of utmost importance is a free and open mind that is curious and a subtle shift in our thinking and perceiving. Jnana yoga gets to be hard for some people because we are using our minds to transcend the mind (itself). Jnana yoga is when I stopped pointing my finger at the world or people as the source of my problems and came to the understanding and realization that only I (my ego) can be the source of "all" my problems. What is in me that needs to shift (or heal), that is causing what is arising in me as an emotion or problem right now triggered by another?

Till we lose or transcend ourselves (our ego), reality (God within) can't be realized or experienced. It is always one (ego) or the other (God)—both can't stay present within us as an experience at the same time.

Ramana adds, "Realization is nothing to be gained anew."[4] All we have to do is to remove, dissolve, or transcend all our conditioning (our mental plus emotional garbage within) via self-inquiry (or other yoga methods mentioned earlier) to realize our true, inherent, primordial nature of pure perfection and wholeness within. That is who I am and who you are to start with. It is what the Taoists call our "natural" state. The nature of this "natural" state is Sat-Chit-Ananda.

What is the state of Sat-Chit-Ananda?

It is the innate knowing in our hearts that we are all one and treating people in such ways in our daily interactions. It is a welling up of unconditional love from within that desires to be shared equally—humility, compassion, empathy, perpetual happiness, and selfless actions toward one and all. This is the state of being in Sat (truth), Chit (knowledge), Ananda (bliss). This is the nature of our primordial state. Each one of us.

As Ramana reminds us, "The real state must be effortless. It is permanent."[5] Once we get anchored in self-realization, we don't have to worry that we will lose it or that it will fade away with time. If it is real, it is permanent.

As a last observation, I would also like to mention that the Vedantic teachings often ascribed to Ramana like, You are That, I am That, You are Brahman, and so forth are coming from Upanishadic times, much before Ramana's. No teachings show up in a vacuum, as we know. Everything is built upon, layered upon, with increased clarity, over time. This is in fact true of everyone's teachings I have discussed in the book.

To sum up this chapter, I will say from my own direct experience that *vichara* (self-inquiry) is the shortest route to *vairagya* (detachment, dispassion, contentment). The method of self-inquiry, Jnana yoga, is the fastest way to gain liberation.

CHAPTER 10

Kabir

Kabir has long been a great source of inspiration for me. He was a poor Muslim weaver who lived in the neglected back quarters of the holy city of Varanasi in Northeast India. His teachings via songs he used to sing were simple, profound, and extremely elegant because they came from his heart. They have survived close to five hundred years since his death. Because he became so popular during his time, and since he used to live in the holy Hindu city of Varanasi, many Hindus started believing that he was actually a Hindu, not a Muslim. During his time, many in the established upper classes of both Hindu and Muslim priestly orders disliked him because his simple ways threatened their rigid and ritualistic ways of religious dogma and belief. As his popularity rose, both Hindus and Muslims became his students or disciples—a rare feat in India then or now. At his death they started arguing over how to perform the last rites on his body—the Hindus wanted to cremate him, while the Muslims wanted to bury him. It is said that when one of the attendants lifted the white sheet covering his body, all they found were flowers, which both sides divided and went on their way. The last part seems to be a story but a nice one.

Kabir's passion was to awaken. He was a Bhakti yogi who through his devotion and love of God within achieved liberation. This love of God within, like the Sufis, he wrote about and expressed in his devotional songs. Kabir believed in the "direct experiencing" of the source within each of us. He urges us to "drink" from those waters. In his many poems, he even mocks the traditional ortho-dox religious heads of both Hindus and Muslims as high priests who keep doing their rituals and outward show-ings of God knowledge but inwardly stay poor and bereft of God. He laments and asks of us again and again, what kind of life are you leading that is devoid of this God (love) connection within? In one of his often-quoted poems, he asks the same questions in this manner:

Are you looking for me? I am in the next seat. My shoulder is against yours.

You will not find me in stupas, not in Indian shrine rooms, nor in synagogues, nor in cathedrals:

not in masses, nor in kirtans, not in legs wind-ing around your neck, nor in eating nothing but vegetables.

You Are Love

When you really look for me, you will see me
instantly—
you will find me in the tiniest house of time.

Kabir says: Student, tell me, what is God?
He is the breath inside the breath.[1]

He kept urging people to awaken to the possibility of a
God connection within, through our own self-efforts and
resulting direct experience.

Jesus, in fact, had the same basic message articulated
so well in Logion 3 of the Gospel of Thomas regarding
the kingdom of God as being within us and that it is only
through our own efforts of knowing and understanding
ourselves in our daily actions that we can find the kingdom within:

If those who lead you say to you "see the kingdom
is in the sky" then birds of the sky will precede
you. If they say to you "It is in the sea" then the fish
of the sea will precede you; Rather, the Kingdom
is inside you and outside you. When you come to
know yourself, then you will become known and
you will realize that it is you who are the sons and
daughters of the living Father. But if you will not
know yourself, you dwell in poverty, and it is you
who are that poverty.[2]

Kabir was not even satisfied just by the repetition of a holy name. He used to mock the Hindus for believing that simply repeating the word *Ram* would get them liberation:

> "Ram! Ram!" they cry,
> till there's a callus on their tongue.
>
> If saying Ram gave liberation,
> saying candy made your mouth sweet,
> saying fire burned your feet,
> saying water quenched your thirst,
> saying food banished hunger,
> the whole world would be free.[3]

I will leave this chapter on Kabir with his urgent message of our need of getting to the end (i.e., our flowering in the here and now, in this life itself) so we don't have to keep coming back:

> Dying, dying, the world keeps dying,
> but none knows how to die.
> No one dies in such a way,
> that he won't die again.[4]

CHAPTER 11

Near-Death Experiences
and the Spirit World

BY THE TIME 2009 was coming to an end, I got to read Raymond Moody's best seller *Life after Life* and got hooked on the near-death-experience (NDE) phenomenon. I was really curious about the spirit world and wanted to research and find out for myself if there indeed is life after death, so I started reading a lot more books about NDEs. In the last two months of 2009, I read five books on NDEs by Raymond Moody and Melvin Morse, who also came to very similar conclusions as Moody on the nature of the near-death experience, but in children.

I excitedly mentioned what I was reading and discovering to so many people I knew. Most didn't care about the topic or didn't want to talk about it. To me, what could be more important than understanding more about our upcoming death, the dying process, and finding out, if possible, the existence or proof of life after death? A friend of mine I used to spin with at the Bay Club, on my nudging, ended up buying the book. I checked with him a couple of weeks later, when I ran into him at the grocery store, and he told me he just couldn't proceed with the book after he understood what it was about. Our already made-up and closed minds are our biggest impediments to our continual learning and self-growth.

The undeniable fact is, we are alive today and will indeed die tomorrow. Should we not find out what that would be like? Surely if I am American and want to move to say Peru, I would indeed inquire about the weather, the customs of the people living in Peru, what kind of foods are available there, and other general information about the area that might make my stay more comfortable and meaningful. Doing research about the afterlife and the spirit world sounded no different to me. Actually, all the more necessary and important. My curiosity also demanded that, at a minimum, I should thoroughly research this area with an open mind and see where it took me. If it took me to a place that didn't make sense to me, I would simply reject it then, not at the start of my search as my friend had done.

It was after reading the elaborate research done by regression therapist Michael Newton that he shared in his groundbreaking book *Journey of Souls,* in very early 2010, that I knew I was onto something of a discovery for myself in my quest to know my answers within and without. That book completely shifted me, or should I say the reading of the last six books in conjunction did. Something clicked deeply within me, to know that this was the truth of how things indeed played out. *Journey of Souls* is about how the spirit world is set up and operates and our continual role in it.

I do want to add here that it would be another almost four years before I would read *Between Death and Life* by Dolores Cannon. In my mind, she reached similar conclusions about the spirit world, its functioning, and our repeated role in it as did Michael Newton. Her book came out a year earlier than Michael's though. She has also written two amazing books via her similar regression work about the life of Jesus and his early ministry that I highly recommend.

I read about Anita Moorjani's story and read her book that became a best seller when it came out. Here was the true story of a woman who had late-stage cancer that gets cured while in a coma as she slips through a tunnel into the spirit world and encounters her NDE phenomenon. She encounters her deceased father and decides to come back to share her story of hope and healing.

Then I read *Proof of Heaven* by Dr. Alexander, a remarkable true story of the workings of the spirit world that he was allowed to witness and experience during his short stay there while he was in coma medically and technically dead. Here was an eminent neurosurgeon and his amazing story. He had no reason to lie or falsify any facts that he must have experienced along the way.

I still remember reading both of these books back to back in less than ten days straight. I was so excited about my new personal growth and learning. A new door had been opened.

When so many people showed up at the same place and arrived at the same conclusions, not even knowing each other and starting at different times and vantage points, I knew it all had to be true. This was also the ecstatic experiences of the ancient Indian yogis of *The Upanishads* who, over three thousand years ago, talked about the nature of reality via their deep meditative states. To me we were coming full circle in our knowledge of the nature of our universe and our role in propagating it.

When Yogananda experienced Yukteswar's physical materialization in the Bombay hotel room where he was staying, as he relates in his autobiography, his guru even talked about the existence of a spirit world and our continued journey of life after death in ever higher realms of learning and growth. In one such higher sphere or dimension is where Yukteswar tells Yogananda, in his book, that he is currently helping spirits to continue on their further evolution and spiritual growth.

The same basic message was showing up wherever I looked with an open mind.

The primary reason I was so excited about my new stepped-up learning and spiritual expansion was the implication of all this in how I needed to live my remaining life on earth. That was the most important part of all this learning for me. If what was being discovered as narrated by those with NDEs after they were resuscitated or by clients in hypnosis during their regression therapy sessions was true, it implied I needed to live my remaining life as well as I could with compassion, care, and love toward one and all I encountered every day, including myself.

Indeed, my state of mind at death would determine which higher sphere of learning and vibration I would get to land on and live in. But to die well, I had to learn to live well.

I remember buying a couple copies of the book *Journey of Souls* for my childhood friends Abhinav in Delhi and Toni in Chandigarh. I needed to share my discovery and excitement with my childhood friends.

I also bought copies for friends and classmates from years ago when I went for my Thapar Engineering College twenty-five-year reunion in the fall of 2010.

Part Four: On Solid Ground—Mill Valley

Years of 2010 through 2015

CHAPTER 12

The Sufi Mystics, Drunk
with Love of God

ON MY FIRST trip to India in early 2010, I was resting under a tree by the side of a small Dargah, an Islamic shrine usually built over a grave of a famous Sufi saint in Delhi. I have always gotten a lot of pull from Sufi saints.

I remembered noticing a fakir (poor ascetic) sitting nearby smoking. I smiled at him, and he nodded back. He asked me to come close-by and inquired if I was a Muslim. I said I lived in the United States and in this life grew up as a Hindu. He liked my answer and laughed. Then he became quiet and didn't say anything, so I asked him who he was and what he was seeking. This chapter is my summary of how he replied to those two questions and more questions I asked over the next half hour.

Often between sentences he would just close his eyes and keep talking as if downloading some higher wisdom from a different realm. He told me he was an educated man who had decided to become a renunciant. Born of a Muslim family in Agra, Salim read about Sufis and was drawn to their way of thinking and living. He said it was his destiny. I was later to learn that Sufis believed in destiny and God's will and their complete surrender to his will. Not even a leaf moves without his will, he told me.

Salim said he spent many years trying to free himself from whatever was not Allah within him. I think he was trying to imply that he had to walk away from everything that tied him to this world, his relationships and worldly stuff—what I would label as our ego-oriented stuff, our me and mine. He said he decided to leave his parents' house many years ago and was now a drifter living off the will and guidance of God. He closed his eyes one more time and said that all human suffering is because of our lack of union with Allah. In response to my question if Allah is outside or inside him, he simply said, both—Allah is everywhere and in everything.

He said, to find Allah we have to empty our hearts of everything; otherwise, he doesn't come.

He added that the key question the Sufi continually asks of himself is, *How open is my heart to his people? How pure is my longing for God?* For a Sufi knows his cleverness or shrewdness as a human being will not bring him an inch closer to God.

I looked at my watch and knew my sister Rita and her husband Raj Singh would be waiting for me at their house.

Salim looked at me and asked me what I was doing at the Dargah being a Hindu. I reassured him that I didn't look at life or people as neatly divided up into Hindus,

Muslims, or Jews. We are all human beings first, I remember saying, and told him that I liked visiting Dargahs because it soothed my heart. I felt the same when I went to a church, I told him.

He then told me a story of a Sufi saint who got tired of not finding God this way or that way, through all his efforts and company of various orders of learned people around him. He then finally pleaded to Allah, "What is the way to you?"

He hears Allah reply, "Just leave yourself and come."

He closed his eyes one more time and said that there were two ways of worshipping Allah: one with our lips and one from our hearts.

He started to gather his belongings, a small bag, and a couple of other small things around him. I reached for my pocket, gave him two five-hundred-rupee notes. He smiled and blessed me. I noticed he probably hadn't taken a shower in quite a while. I asked him where he was headed and if I could drop him, in my taxi, somewhere. He told me he didn't know, that he was just passing through.

On getting back from that trip, I dived deeper into Sufism. I read about Rumi; Hafiz; Kabir; Farid Attar; Maneri, the Indian Sufi who lived in a forest in Bihar in the thirteenth century; Junayd; Rabia, the eighth-century Muslim woman mystic based in Basra, Iraq; and many others.

It is said of Rabia that she was a beautiful girl who was sold as a slave to a master who would prostitute her. She was also physically and sexually abused from an early age.

One night the master saw that there was a very beautiful light emanating from the quarter where Rabia used to be holed up. He peeked in and saw that while Rabia was in prayer kneeling down, there was light surrounding her. He knew then that Rabia had a higher connection with God, and the next day he released her from his captivity. It is said that Rabia, by now in her late forties, went into the desert and started living a quiet life in meditation and prayer in a hut by a small community.

Soon she started receiving visitors seeking her spiritual guidance and healing abilities. There is a story attributed to her that goes something like this:

> Once she cured a rich man who offered her a bag of gold coins. She is said to have thrown it outside, saying, "Dear, if you leave that, flies will gather as if a horse just relieved himself, and I might slip in it while dancing."[1]

There is a beautiful poem of Rabia titled "In My Soul," translated by Daniel Ladinsky in his book *Love Poems from God*:

> In my soul there is a temple, a shrine, a mosque, a church where I kneel.
> Prayer should bring us to an altar where no walls or names exist.

Is there not a region of love where the sovereignty
is illuminated nothing,
Where ecstasy gets poured into itself and becomes lost,
Where the wing is fully alive but has no mind or
body?
In my soul there is a temple, a shrine, a mosque,
a church
That dissolves, that dissolves in God.[2]

Rumi was born over four hundred years after the death of
Rabia, and she is said to have influenced his writings along
with, of course, Shams of Tabriz, his teacher. All the great
Sufi saints who came after her, like Farid Attar of Persia,
Junayd, and Al-Ghazali, continued to hold her in high re-
gard and esteem.

The singular focus of a Sufi, then, is the union with
God within and without, the highest purpose of life. The
"removal of everything that is not God within" is our process of transcending our ignorance or ego. One can then
continue to live and thrive in the world equanimously. We
don't have to become a renunciant or abandon society or
our relationships.

CHAPTER 13

Calcutta Trip, December 2010

I VERY MUCH wanted to visit and experience the energy at the various sacred places mentioned in the autobiography of Yogananda as well as the various Mother Teresa centers in Calcutta. Since I had finished reading Ramakrishna by then as well, I wanted to visit his main ashram, also by Calcutta, and the famous temple where he resided and was the temple priest for many years. I had also been supporting many kids in Calcutta through Children's International, the charity organization based in Kansas, and wanted to visit them as well. I and my then girlfriend, Shelly, decided to take a trip to India.

The first thing I noticed landing at Calcutta airport was how dirty it was and that nobody seemed to care. I grew up in India, but even for me it was dirty. We were staying at the Oberoi Hotel in the city. Interestingly enough, by the third or fourth day, we simply got used to it. The Indian food at the hotel was probably the best we had during that whole trip.

We were flying in from Delhi after staying in Agra for about four days. Sitting outside and looking at the Taj

Mahal every day from our hotel patio room was simply majestic. Every morning, it was so peaceful to hear the call to prayer for the Muslims from a nearby mosque and religious Hindu songs emanating from a local nearby temple. One was transported to a time long gone by.

We were in Calcutta for six full days in which our goal was to cover the major SRF- and YSS-related ashrams and notable places to visit; see the Ramakrishna- and Vivekananda-related places of our interest; visit Mother Teresa's various homes, the Children's International centers in Calcutta, and, time permitting, the museum of Rabindranath Tagore, the famous Nobel Prize-winning poet and ascetic in the city.

Well before getting to Calcutta to maximize my take-in experience, I had pretty much read all I wanted to about the various organizations we were going to visit.

I still remember how I got to know of Ramakrishna. I had enrolled in a weekend course at the California Institute of Integral Studies in San Francisco. This was in early 2009. During one of the breaks, I ended up talking with Sally, the teacher, about her journey with Muktananda, whose disciple she was while living in India. I mentioned then that I was involved with Yogananda and the Self Realization Fellowship (SRF) organization and was planning to visit his childhood home in Calcutta later that year. She mentioned about Ramakrishna as another sage also close to Calcutta that I should look into. Ever curious, I asked her for a book recommendation on him, and she recommended his famous book, *Ramakrishna and His Disciples*, by Christopher Isherwood. I came home, looked at the Amazon reviews, and received the book on April 16. I started reading it on May 5 and finished it on May 16 and found it to be an amazing read on Ramakrishna and his mission. I also found a photo of him, got it framed, and Ramakrishna became a part of my altar. I had much to learn from this great Indian sage.

The first fresh day in Calcutta, we decided to visit the Dakshineshwar Temple of Kali outside of Calcutta, where Ramakrishna started as a temple priest when he was a young man of nineteen and lived there for many years. From a young age, Ramakrishna would go into a trance very easily. As he started his priestly duties at the Kali Temple, built by a rich lady by the name of Rani Rasmani in 1855, his ecstatic states would only amp up. During some of his daily priestly puja performances, he would simply fall on the floor in ecstasy of the mother Kali, tears pouring down his face to the extent that the temple authorities got very worried about Ramakrishna's mental and emotional state. Disregarding how he looked or what he wore, he was always absorbed in the love of God. Often he would pray to God as if he was a Muslim or as a Christian in his demeanor and prayers. He saw God in everything and everyone.

Ramakrishna soon started attracting his core disciples, the foremost of them being Vivekananda, whom he trained and loved very much. It was Vivekananda who traveled to the United States in 1893, after Ramakrishna's death in 1886, to spread the message of Vedanta and Hinduism. He and a band of loyal disciples of Ramakrishna also later formalized and started, in Calcutta, a religious organization around their guru and his teachings in 1897, what is today known worldwide as the Ramakrishna Mission. Before coming on this visit to Calcutta, I also stopped by the Ramakrishna Mission chapter on Vallejo Street in San Francisco. It was there on one of my subsequent visits, while I was talking to the lady running the library well stocked with books of all sorts and music, that I learned that the famous Dakshineshwar Kali Temple of Calcutta, where Ramakrishna spent most of his adult life, is not under the Belur Math- or Ramakrishna-organization umbrella. I was looking for the aarti (*puja*) music that they play at the Kali Temple in Calcutta that I had just come back from visiting, and the lady mentioned that "they" play different aarti music than we do. I thanked her for sharing that technicality and ended up buying some books on Rumi.

The most profound experience I witnessed at the Dakshineshwar Kali Temple on that visit was while I was sitting in the room where Ramakrishna used to stay in the temple and have his disciples present. The room is as is, with Ramakrishna's bed still there, old photos hanging on the wall, and his other memorabilia. The whole temple was very crowded that day as was this room. There was a priest sitting on the floor toward one corner of the room, and there was a narrow human-made path in front of him that devotees were snaking through as they walked the room. I didn't want to leave so quickly in the moving line and decided to quietly sit, almost facing the priest, with my back against the other side of the wall. The smell of burning incense and the abundance of beautiful-smelling marigolds in the room felt very intoxicating to me. I had closed my eyes by then. As the priest gently and in slow motion rocked his hand holding a hand bell and kept softly humming some Sanskrit mantras, which I didn't quite understand, my heart just tore open within me. I started crying with uncontrollable joy. The priest caught my eye a couple of times and sweetly smiled. As I write this close to five years later, I can simply close my eyes and just be there. Such experiences are so profound that they get etched in our psyche. We can access them anytime. There was so much love in that room, I couldn't get up. Finally, realizing that Shelly might be waiting outside, I left the room, after depositing some money in the deposit box in front of me, to find Shelly chatting with Raju (our driver), whose car we had rented at the hotel before we left. We used Raju's services for our entire stay. He was a really sweet man, but his car, an old beat-up ambassador, was hard to be in for too long.

After sharing between the three of us some lunch that we had brought from the hotel, we sat on a small boat to head to Belur Math, the headquarters of the Ramakrishna Mission. It was a bit further up and on the other side of the

Ganges River. As we settled down with about twenty-five other people on this small boat, I saw that Raju was very uncomfortable. I asked him what was going on, and we all started laughing when he told me that this was his first time on a boat.

Belur Math was a quieter place and very clean. We first went to the bookstore, where I bought some books of Vivekananda and couple of photos of Ramakrishna; his wife, Sarada Devi, who was also a saint of a high order; and goddess Kali as additions to my growing altar at home. We walked around the campus for a bit, saw the main temple of Ramakrishna, and went into a separate house that used to be where Vivekananda lived. The campus, with the quietly flowing Ganges next to it, felt so beautiful to take in. As we sat to take some rest under a tree, the periodic ringing of a hanging bell at the entrance of a nearby temple just added to the harmony and joy we were experiencing within.

From there, on the way back to our hotel, we had time to stop over and see the headquarters of the Yogoda Satsang Society (YSS) of India, the Indian arm of Yogananda's Self Realization Fellowship based out of Los Angeles. Yogananda dedicated this facility, also on the holy Ganges, on his visit back to India in 1939. We walked around the beautiful gardens and meditated a bit, and then I went into the office to find out if it was possible to visit the childhood home of Yogananda in Calcutta as mentioned in the autobiography. The gentleman at the desk in the office gave me a telephone number of a lady at the house, a Mrs. Sarita Ghosh, a relative of Yogananda. We called her upon getting back to our hotel that evening and set up an appointment to visit the house the next evening once she got back from work.

The next day, after our workout in the hotel gym, we got dressed and had a quick breakfast, and with a packed lunch, we headed out to Serampore, about thirty kilometers from our hotel, which would take us at least one hour and thirty minutes each way. I had asked Raju to see if he could find a better car with a working air conditioner so we could close the windows, still be able to breathe, and keep the dirt and smoke outside the car. That was always a challenge in his beat-up ambassador. To our surprise he had a newer-looking white Maruti and was waiting with a big smile on his face. He introduced us to his older brother, whose car he had borrowed, and we set out.

The location we were heading to used to be Yukteswar's house, serving as an ashram where he used to train his disciples, including Yogananda. Over the years after his death, the larger house apparently got divided into smaller portions within his remaining family, and the small temple we ended up going to is the part that YSS owned. We disembarked from our car outside and walked through the solid metal gates and into the temple. The front-facing wall as we walked through the metal meshed doors, common in India, had the standard six photos of the six SRF yogis: Jesus and Krishna in the middle, Yogananda and Yukteswar on the right of them, and Lahiri Mahasaya and Babaji on the left respectively. I noticed an older gentleman as the only other guy sitting quietly meditating. We sat down sort of in the middle of the room facing the wall-mounted SRF altar. I noticed toward my left was a white marble bust of Yukteswar sitting on a brownish marble pedestal. We had told Raju that we wouldn't be too long. I closed my eyes to meditate for a bit. No sooner had I done so that I felt a charge of energy sweep over me. Slowly, I started gently rocking back and forth without any effort on my part. After that went on for some time, I recall a humming sound that started emanating from me, again with no effort on my part. I could clearly hear the passing traffic on the road as well as kids playing and making noise. But I could not open my eyes even if I tried. It was almost like an energy had taken over me and was in full control. My rocking became deeper as did my humming from my throat. I had tears of unconditional love and joy flowing down my cheeks. This went on for one hour and fifteen minutes, and by the time I opened my eyes, I was almost facing Yukteswar's bust. Apparently, I had moved almost ninety degrees in this process of rocking and humming, toward Yukteswar. The best way I can describe that experience is that I was completely emptied and washed over with love.

We walked outside, into the sun. I was so moved that when I saw Raju, our driver, I gave him one hundred rupees from my pocket and told him to go inside, put it in the donation box, and ask for a blessing for himself and his family, which he did.

Every time I look at Yogananda, I experience unconditional love emanating from him. From Yukteswar, I feel strength, protection, and guidance. I will fast-forward here to an experience that occurred in 2014 at the house in Mill Valley, where I have been staying for the past two years now. As 2014 was coming to an end, I was a practicing Reiki healer and often would give healing to my friends without charge. On one such occasion, my friend Susan came over for a short joint meditation session of about twenty minutes, and then I was going to give her an energy-healing session to clear out any energy blocks she might be holding on to unknowingly. Such sessions can last about thirty to forty-five minutes depending on the person and how much needs to be cleared.

Essentially, our daily stress, if not cleared regularly, manifests as energy blockages within us that over time starts to hamper the flow of universal energy, or *prana*, through our body. This accumulated stress within us over time results in our physical disease. The basic purpose of having a daily meditation practice is to simply remove or dissolve such energy blockages within us.

Once I got done with the energy clearing, I asked Susan how she felt, and she mentioned, pointing to Yukteswar's framed photo on my altar, that she saw this bearded guy in her mind's eye as she lay there with her eyes closed. Now, up until this point, Susan, who had been to my house once before for a similar Reiki session, had never inquired about any of the many bearded guys on my altar, and I generally don't say anything unless asked. I just introduce new people to my altar by saying something like, *These guys are here to help and guide us, so let's just stay open to their energy.* She then added that she also saw a lion with him. That got my attention. Yukteswar was such a strong and fully realized yogi when alive that Yogananda used to call him Bengal's lion, and he mentions this in his autobiography as well. Talk about quantum nonlocal communication.

Before Susan left, I told her to go on the SRF website, buy a photo of Yukteswar, get it framed, and start an altar at her house with him. He was calling her.

Once finished with Yukteswar's hermitage on the way out, we stopped by the big banyan tree by the Ganges where Babaji, the eternal living Siddha yogi, came to visit Yukteswar after he finished writing his book, *The Holy Science*, as mentioned in the autobiography.

We headed back to our hotel to take a quick shower, have dinner, and then go visit the ancestral home at 4 Garpar Road where Yogananda spent his early years and is now the residence of his brother's grandson, Somnath Ghosh, his wife, Sarita Ghosh, and their two kids.

I want to also mention briefly here that Sananda Lal Ghosh, the five-year younger brother of Yogananda—whom he lovingly used to call Mejda—wrote the really informative book also called *Mejda* about the early years and adventures of Yogananda. It is a really amazing read if the reader wants to truly understand the "making" of Yogananda. I will just highlight a few notable things I found very interesting and similar in the context of the broader themes I have covered in this book about the existence of the spirit world, the reality of psychic phenomenon, and the phenomenon of physical materializations.

Mejda practiced mediumship early on through his younger brother, was able to contact their dead mother in the astral world through Sananda Lal, used to go for day-long meditations at the Dakshineswar Kali Temple where Ramakrishna used to be the priest when alive, used to meditate under the same Panchavati tree that Ramakrishna got illumination under, and used to hang out and meditate in cremation grounds, like Indian Tantric saints still do, all to accelerate his destined spiritual awakening.

In the book, Sananda Lal also mentions an encounter at a schoolhouse where a headmaster by the name of Mahendra Gupta used to live. This is the same Mahendra or "M" who wrote *The Gospel of Sri Ramakrishna*, the famous book of that great being of light. He was a high-caliber meditative adept who was an ardent devotee of the goddess Kali, like Ramakrishna himself. On one occasion, Sananda Lal recalls sitting quietly in M's room, both him and Mejda, behind M, facing his altar with a photo of Kali. He recalls then seeing the eyes of goddess Kali move in that photo.

Mahendra was such a high-order spiritual adept that once Mejda and his younger brother requested of Mahendra to manifest their mother from the astral world. Sananda then describes in the book that they sat for two hours quietly behind Mahendra who was in deep meditation the whole time. Soon then, he softly told them to turn and see who was standing behind them. Both Yogananda and his younger brother turned to find their dear mother fully materialized standing in the doorway smiling at them. She looked radiant and happy and told them that she keeps constant watch over them as does the divine mother, implying the goddess Kali.

This book *Mejda* is a treasure. Sananda Lal had felt after the autobiography came out that there were so many wonderful stories not covered in that book and thus felt the need to write *Mejda* to complete the story of Yogananda, which he barely got to finish before passing in 1979, at the age of eighty-one. Sananda Lal is that same younger brother of Yogananda whose many beautiful paintings are hung at the SRF Mother Center, at Hollywood Temple, and other SRF locations.

I had checked with the hotel concierges to find out that the house on 4 Garpar Lane was in the northern part of Calcutta, near Raja Bazar, about twenty to thirty minutes from our hotel. I again checked with Sarita, and we set up a time of seven in the evening.

We promptly rung the bell at our allocated time, and Sarita opened the door and wholly welcomed us inside.

We went first to the small attic room upstairs to the side of the house, described by Yogananda in his autobiography where in his very early spiritual formation years on the instance of a Tantric Sadhu, to deepen his sadhana, had placed a human skull and two human bones crosswise to meditate on at his altar for a couple of days, as Tantrics usually do, to accelerate his flowering.

Sananda Lal in his book *Mejda*, recalls going up to this attic room one day to find the skull had the same deep vermilion mark as on this Sadhu's forehead, whose eyes were always red, who used to visit their home with Mejda. This is also the same attic room where Yogananda later said he found God. Shortly thereafter, on the polite insistence of his father, Mejda stopped this type of meditative sadhana.

I love the fact that Yogananda was so open and hungry spiritually to try different ways to accelerate his spiritual flowering. In my mind this hunger within for union with our higher self is essential for our flowering to take place. This was all before Mejda was to meet his destined guru, Yukteswar, whom he had known for many lifetimes.

We each sat in meditation for about fifteen minutes, as the attic would have been a squeeze for two at the same time. We then went to a couple of other rooms in the house and saw various old photos of Yogananda, sofas he sat on, and beds he meditated or used to sleep on. The whole house is maintained as a beautiful shrine of Yogananda. It was a really warm and welcoming experience for both of us. On the way out, we were also offered a Prasad (offering) of some Indian sweetmeats. There was a small nondescript-looking donation box in the attic where I had gently left our donations. Overall, it was a beautiful experience to visit Yogananda's childhood home.

The next day was spent visiting the various centers of Mother Teresa. Having been involved with Mother Teresa in San Francisco by now, I was really looking forward to these tours of some of the homes. We started at the Mother House, where her tomb is. There was also a sort of museum display by the side in a couple of rooms tracing some of the history of Mother Teresa and her work. The atmosphere was so filled with love, gratitude, and a feeling of abiding peace as the candles stayed lit quietly in acknowledgment.

The sisters in their white saris with blue borders were going about their daily chores of washing clothes and pulling water, almost oblivious to the visitors moving around curiously. We sat on a bench by her tomb. I was overwhelmed and just closed my eyes. After a short time, we walked by her very spartan room with a simple bed on one side by the wall and a wooden table and bench as her work space in a rather small room where she lived and worked for over forty years, till her death on September 5, 1997.

The main office to deposit any donations was right by the corner there, and I wanted to give some money before we moved to the next of her locations. We had to wait a good twenty minutes because there were people ahead of us in line who wanted to do the same thing.

Just down the road was a children's home called Nirmala Shishu Bhavan. There were kids aged anywhere from two or three and up. It was noisy with the chatter of kids and their activities. We looked around for some time in the kitchen and playground areas and left.

After a quick, rather late lunch at the hotel, we headed out to see another Kali temple, called Kalighat Kali Temple on the other side of town. I was also hoping to visit the Mother Teresa center next door, called Nirmal Hriday, the home of the dying destitutes. To avoid getting sick on the journey, we would only eat our meals at the hotel. There was so much to cover, and the last thing I wanted was a sickness to slow us down.

This Kali temple experience was something new, even for me who had grown up in India. After the ambassador car dropped us a half a kilometer from the temple, we started getting accosted rather aggressively by people who wanted to hang on to our shoes and expected us to walk the rest of the way to the temple barefoot on grounds that were truly filthy. I could see dog poop everywhere. I also saw some homeless and very sick old people lying spread out all over the entrance area. They were so incapacitated that they couldn't move around and had to simply turn over to pee. It was a very difficult way to try and enter a temple for sure. We didn't want to get any sort of infection through our bare feet. We just kept walking past all the people. Once on the temple grounds, a guy walked up to me, knowing full well that I was not a foreigner—at least I didn't look it—and almost ordered us to sit on one of the side benches there. He took our shoes and hid there somewhere. Shelly didn't want to get into the big crowd to get a *darshan* (view) of the idol of Kali in the main temple. I was asked without choice to come up and fight the crowd to get through. Once in front of the Kali idol, I folded my hands and started to turn around to leave, when the younger-looking temple priest standing by the idol caught me by my shirt and asked for money. I said I didn't have any in my pocket, which was true. I didn't want to be pickpocketed and had left my wallet behind. He wouldn't let me go. I was pretty upset by then. I just couldn't believe I was being heckled like that at a place of worship. Unfortunately, some temples in India do this.

After getting back to where Shelly was sitting, I got my wallet and gave another of his fellow temple juniors who followed me back down the stairs five hundred rupees to get him off my back. We got our shoes, and as we were walking out, another guy asked me if we wanted to see some holy Ganges water and a sacred murti (idol) of Shiva. I am not sure why I ended up following him into another area of the temple, quiet and cut off from everyone. There were two of these temple priests and just the two of us. They closed the heavy doors once we were inside. I instantly felt trapped. They pointed to a pond with really dirty and murky green water as a fresh inlet of the Ganges holy water. I knew they were blatantly lying. There was a white marble idol of Shiva where they did some puja, another excuse to extract some money from us. We had to get out, so I gave them two thousand rupees, one thousand for each of us, and we bolted from there. That was a really bad experience. Living in India all my years till I was twenty-one years old, when I left to come to the United States to do my MBA, I had never experienced this kind of aggressive behavior in a place of worship. It was almost like the temple had to make their number for the month or quarter. Funnily enough, we read in the local paper the next morning that enough foreigners had complained about this temple that they had beefed up more police security around it from that day on.

All this drama made us miss our visit next door to the Mother Teresa center I really wanted to visit. It closed by the time we got there. Not meant to be.

We spent the next two days with the US-based (Kansas) charity organization, Children International, that I had been involved in since 2003 and Shelly got involved in once we met in 2009. By 2010 we were supporting fifteen children through the organization, I ten and Shelly five. Basically, when we sponsored a child, our support would pay for the child's basic health, dental and general nutritional-care needs, school supplies, medicine, and youth-program education and guidance. That is what generally got covered in our twenty-two dollars per child per month. Lots of these kids have parents but are poor enough that they can't afford to take care of such needs that get fulfilled through local chapters of this great organization worldwide.

Over the years, I had really admired this charity's work and wanted to support them more. How this encounter got started, if I remember correctly, was in 2003, when we were living in Westport, Connecticut, and I was working in Manhattan at a market-neutral hedge fund. I had just finished a quick lunch and was heading back to the office on Fifty-Second Street when I ran into this young guy on the side of the street who started pitching to me to support kids worldwide through this organization he was promoting. I looked at the kid's photo and decided to support a child in Calcutta. From that one child, I grew my support to around ten kids over the years. I remember in 2010, on my birthday, I asked Shelly to support a child as my birthday present, which she gladly did.

For our welcome the local chapter and their director had organized a really nice lunch where we got to meet most of our sponsored children with their parents. Some of them had to travel quite a way to attend the lunch. There was a nice Indian tent pitched on the roof of one of the center buildings where we all sat and had a wonderful lunch. Shelly had brought some little items as giveaways for the kids—cool-looking pencils, erasers, funny-looking sharpeners—which she handed to them one by one. We took photos with each child. It was really great and fulfilling for everyone to meet each other and for us to put faces to names as we used to receive monthly updates and progress reports on each kid.

The next day, we toured some of the centers and were pretty impressed by the amount of support each of such centers provided, including computer support for making résumés and finding jobs for senior high-school kids as they had moved up in the system. Each center, being in a poor and often neglected part of a neighborhood, would end up serving as a nerve center and activity hub for everybody involved, kids and the rest of their families.

The last day, we spent leisurely touring Rabindranath Tagore's house, which, since his death, had become a museum in his honor. Beautiful and stately, I thought it really fit Tagore and his legacy as the first Indian Noble Prize winner, in 1913, for literature. I also remembered reading a translation he had done of some of Kabir's songs that was really well done.

In the afternoon on our last full day in Calcutta, we stopped by Vivekananda's stately ancestral house in Calcutta. Vivekananda came from a very well-to-do family, and then everything changed for him as in his youth he came to acquaint with Ramakrishna, who was to become his guru. Vivekananda, though, initially didn't take well to Ramakrishna's sweet overtures. Ramakrishna, who knew Vivekananda to be his first and most committed of disciples when they initially met, playfully ignored Vivekananda's childlike resistance.

Vivekananda kept visiting halfheartedly the Kali temple in Dakshineshwar where this priest was developing a liking for him, though he couldn't understand why. Initially, Vivekananda did not fully believe or understand the ecstatic trance states Ramakrishna would suddenly go into till one day Ramakrishna gently touched him on his forehead. Vivekananda lost all consciousness by that simple touch. Then he started to understand his unfolding destiny. Vivekananda was to later walk away from all his family's wealth and reach and tour the whole of India as an ascetic for many months and later was destined to be one of the first Indian yogis of Vedanta to come to America to open that door for the Western audience.

CHAPTER 14

How Wall Street Pounded Spirituality into Me

THE WAY THINGS worked out for me, I only spent my first two years as a research analyst on the sell side. Once I moved to the buy side, there was no going back for me. It was a different kind of challenge, and for me there was nothing better than picking stocks and often being right on stocks I owned.

Over the years since 2006, I have had big up and down years in my personal portfolio that have also played a crucial role in my mind to really hammer home the transitory nature of money and what it buys. It is so easy to make and lose money in the markets, especially when one is unidirectional like I am. Since I have been managing my own money, and greed plays a big role in why we are in the markets in the first place, I have found it oxymoronic to have shorts (betting on certain stocks to go down in price) in a bull market and longs (betting on certain stocks to go up in price) in a bear market. In a bull market, my shorts only slow me down, while in a bear market, it is almost impossible for any of my longs to make me money. The whole point of being in the markets is to make money. It is far easier (as most long-short equity hedge-fund managers already know) to wish for our longs to keep going up in any market and for our shorts to keep going down. Inspite of our best research and intentions, the realities of markets often don't grant us the luxury of contemplative wish. We learn grudgingly and over time that most stocks are at the mercy of the prevailing trend.

Since most stocks go up in bull markets and go down in bear markets, I decided it made more sense to try and figure out first, at any given time, if we are in a bull or a bear market. Now this is no easy task as most on Wall Street know. A lot of people believe it can't be done, that markets can't be (approximately) timed over an economic or stock-market cycle. In my repeated experience, they certainly can be.

In my mind, because most professional investors think that markets can't be timed at all, they tend to employ a strictly bottom-up approach to picking stocks (finding the most favorable stocks based on earnings potential irrespective of concern for bull or bear markets) versus the top-down approach (buying favorable stocks based on earnings potential but only when we are in a bull market) I favor. Also, because it would be hard for professional investors to justify earning their management fees from clients if they parked their funds in cash, is another reason that they stay in the markets, constantly trying to fight it out often without much success. To me, the client is best served when he or she does not lose money in bear markets and makes money in bull markets. Having said all this, I do realize that trying to manage other people's money is an entirely different ball game and stress level than managing one's own. Life is so much easier when we are not answerable to anyone else.

If I am an individual investor not paying much attention to the markets or not having the time or inclination to do so, the best strategy still seems to be to buy the cheapest index Exchange Traded Funds (ETFs) out there and keep deploying periodic monies into them regardless of market movements. If I was not actively involved in the markets, that's what I would be doing.

I go to cash when my work suggests it is the best course for me, like as of this writing. I did the same thing coming into 2008. I stayed out the whole year and did end up missing the early bull market resumption of 2009. I also have made plenty of mistakes and lost plenty of money along the way of perfecting "my art" of trying to make money in the markets. It's clearly a tough game. This is how I have come up with my list of things never to do, mentioned below.

I still do my basic bottom-up research on every name I own long, but I don't constantly obsess over every quarter's earnings report when I know I am in a bull market upswing. Same way, when I know we are heading into a bear market, it is only a matter to time before even the good earnings of a company will get marginalized by the downward pull of the overall trend of the markets. In such instances, why fight it by being long?

This is how I try and make decisions on what to buy and when. I have tailored a style of investing that makes sense for me and leaves me with ample time and energy to pursue other interests and not constantly obsess about every market move. There are many ways to make money in the markets. I respect them all. Each market participant has a different way of looking at the markets, a unique demeanor and appetite for risk. What works for me might not work for the fellow next to me.

Over the ten years now, in light of my way of investing, some rules that I have rigidly been made to follow by the markets are:

- I never do equity options of any kind simply because they keep my mind preoccupied all the time.
- I don't short stocks.
- I don't invest in commodity equity of any kind.
- I never buy two-x or three-x ETFs.
- If I am down 15 to 20 percent in any position at any given time, it doesn't matter how much time I have spent researching the name, how cool the technology sounds, or how much I love the story, I simply get out, knowing full well that I can get

back in another day or that I might just be plain wrong in my analysis in the first place.

HUMILITY IS GRACE in the markets. I have been reminded again and again this, till I finally relented and learned.

° I never have any single long position over 20 percent of the portfolio.

As I said earlier, before picking stocks long at any given time, I first try to do a good amount of fundamental and technical analysis to understand where we are in the current upswing or bull market. For example, as of the writing of this book, toward the middle of November 2015, all my work and research has been suggesting that we are in the early phase of a bear market, and so I am 100 percent in cash. I have been for the past three months. I wish I was even three months earlier than that. I keep accessing my current bearish outlook with how the market unfolds on a daily and weekly basis. All I am doing right now is watching how the market is behaving.

I learn the most from watching how stocks are acting versus the news that is being thrown at each of them. Stock movements have human beings and their emotions behind them. If there are more sellers than buyers in a stock I really like, with the result that it can't hold and build on its gains, I simply let myself get stopped out. I wait for a washout and throw a small line again to see if things might stick at this lower level. Then I repeat again till it starts to stick. This way I try to lose only a limited amount of money each time I try.

My goal of being long in the stock market versus being in cash and not wanting to fight a bear market, trying to be long, is all about managing my emotions and conserving my energy. How much emotion should I attach to my portfolio's daily ups and downs? Our emotions, especially negative ones, deplete our limited daily energy. I also don't want to be thinking about markets all day and night. That is such a drag. This is the biggest challenge I have found being in the markets all the time. It drains my energy when I get caught in its inevitable downswings. Often when things get too hairy and the action of the markets or the individual names I own start acting as if I don't understand their action, I just get out, take rest, and regroup. That time off the treadmill is very essential for me.

Trying to manage my own money over the years has definitely made me humbler and rethink my relationship with money. Clearly, money is important in our lives. I want to live a good life, take care of my kids, and leave something behind for them.

As important as money is to each of us, I look at money now as a commodity much like water, which has a utility, a necessity in my life, but too much of it can also make me delirious. When we drink too much water, we can start feeling delirious due to the lack of sodium in our body that it tends to wash away. In my mind, an obsession with moneymaking can have very similar and real effects on people unless one is detached from its action. There is definitely so much more to life than constantly obsessing about money.

I didn't use to think like this, living in a six thousand-square-foot home in Tiburon, overlooking the ocean and downtown San Francisco till 2006, but I do now. Since then, the faster I woke up to this truth, the happier and truly more fulfilled and connected within I have felt.

So I have to thank my ongoing career on Wall Street to also have contributed immensely in making me more spiritual and whole by forcing me to long for the need for equanimity in my life, which I was subsequently made to learn can only come from detachment to its events, including Wall Street's daily action.

CHAPTER 15

Amritsar Trip, Spring 2011

I HAD NEVER been to see the Golden Temple in Amritsar, the most sacred place for Sikhs, and wanted to go. I also wanted to visit the Jallianwala Bagh (park) in Amritsar where thousands of Hindus and Sikhs, including women and children, were brutally shot at and killed by General Dyer, a British general then posted in British India pre-Independence. That event is shown with its full rawness in the movie *Gandhi* as well.

I had read a couple of books on Sikhism by now and felt ready to visit and experience the beauty and charm of this most sacred Sikh abode.

Growing up in Chandigarh since I was twelve, I had many Sikh friends, including my childhood friend Toni who lived opposite our house. I had been to the Gurdwara (Sikh Temple) many times and often used to listen to Gurbani (the sayings and compositions of various Sikh gurus often sung as melodious songs) at home, as my dad used to like listening to it on his radio on the weekends. I was also much later to learn that a lot of Kabir's (discussed earlier) poems were also a part of such compositions.

Toni had a cool purple-colored four-by-four that we all got into for our road journey to Amritsar—Shelly and I and Toni and his wife, Simrat. We leisurely covered the four-hour journey stopping in between to get a hearty lunch of *parathas* (vegetable-stuffed fried Indian bread), yogurt, and really delicious *kheer* (sweet-milk-soaked cooked rice). On getting to Amritsar, finding a place to stay became a problem. The place we were going to stay ended up being a bit farther away from the temple. With all the rush at the temple pretty much all day, we wanted to stay closer by.

So we stopped by a Sarai (temple-organized place to stay overnight) right next to the temple and inquired within. Toni made some phone calls, and we found our two rooms. Such phone calls work wonders in India. By the time we checked in, put our luggage in the rooms, and headed down to the temple on foot, it was well past sundown, and the temperatures had dropped considerably. I didn't realize Amritsar in February could be this cold. Before entering the temple, we, of course, had to check in our shoes and this made things worse for us. Our feet were freezing already, and we hadn't started our journey in. Walking some distance, we realized that the floors in many areas were wet. We shivered and grunted and kept moving. As we turned the corner, we saw the really long line to get into the main part of the temple, Harmandir Sahib (God's abode). There was a line of people as far as I could see, thousands waiting patiently for their turn to get in. There was a beautiful Gurbani one could hear coming from big loudspeakers all over. By now it was dark, and all the lights were on inside and outside the temple, and it was really beautiful to see the shimmering reflections of the gold-covered Harmandir Sahib in the surrounding waters around it.

Luckily, one of Toni's friends at the temple guided us via a parallel faster way into the temple. I remember being amazed that no one was jumping that long line in spite of the cold. India being what it is with so many people, jumping lines is very common. But not here at God's abode. I thought that was really respectful and beautiful.

Once inside, I sat on the second floor against the wall in a corner in full lotus in meditation for fifteen minutes or so. We had to move out soon because of the incoming traffic. I paid a generous donation, and we were ushered out. Later we stopped by the place in the temple to get *langar*, a free cooked meal served to anyone and everyone who shows up every day. This is probably the best facet of Sikhism I truly admire. The willingness to share food irrespective of religion or faith with strangers to me is so honorable. We sat down to eat on the really cold marble floors. I thought the food was pretty good and saw Shelly with her big scarf over and around her head smiling, acknowledging.

We finished our food, left the room to step outside to get some much-needed hot tea. The tea was hot but way too sweet for me. Indians in India love their really sweet teas. I have always wondered why. I couldn't take more than a couple of sips. I saw Shelly heading back for a refill.

I could tell she was really cold and didn't care much how sweet the tea was. Suddenly, I noticed that Simrat was not with us. On inquiring, Toni told me she was helping clean the dishes we just ate in, in the general dish-cleaning area. This was another really beautiful Sikh custom I thought: everyone, and I mean everyone, pitched in to cook the food and clean the dishes.

By now we were really cold and headed back to our Sarai for a much-needed restful sleep.

The next morning, we visited the close-by Jallianwala Bagh compound. We walked around in the small museum there and on the grounds, and I actually got to see how small and confining that place is. There is still a water well there, in the middle of the grounds and now almost filled up with sand, into which women and children had thrown themselves in panic on April 13, 1919, because they had nowhere else to hide from the oncoming relentless bullets. I'd seen this in the movie *Gandhi*.

There was also only one entrance to get in and out of that park, which was blocked by General Dyer's armored machine-gun van, which he actually intended to take in and shoot from. Luckily, the narrow cement gate didn't allow that, so he had his Indian-army soldiers line up inside and had them start shooting randomly at men, women, and children who had no way to get out, as if they were animals. What a brave guy.

Shortly afterward, we left for Chandigarh, and the next day, Shelly and I left for Delhi.

CHAPTER 16

Jiddu Krishnamurti and
Ojai Trip, Summer 2011

I REMEMBER VISITING a house of a relative from my wife's side when we were still married in 2003 in Arizona. There I first encountered Krishnamurti (K). There was an open book lying face up in the bathroom with a K staring right at me. I tried to go through a couple of pages but couldn't much make sense of what K was trying to get across. I left the book, finished my business, and went on my way.

K can be pretty hard to understand and process. I knew that from my own experience years ago.

The next time I tried to understand him, it wasn't hard. When I read his first book, *The Book of Life*, in 2010, I was deeply impressed by him. The clarity and depth of K's understanding of human nature and behavior that he was putting across was unparalleled to anything I had read till then. I also remember buying a copy of the book for Abhinav, my childhood friend living in Delhi.

Clearly, by the time mid-April 2010 had rolled around, I had cleaned myself enough within to allow K to come in. As time went on, I realized that the more I understood and dissolved my conditioning, the deeper my clarity grew, and the more I could let K in.

Krishnamurti's basic approach of looking at ourselves in full self-awareness in our daily relationships in how we act, behave, and respond can act like a fire that starts to burn our mental and emotional garbage right away. This I can attest to from my own direct experience. I like to call my conditioning garbage so I can keep getting repulsed by it on a daily basis. This increases my desire to dissolve it faster so I can act and behave as a better version of myself on a daily basis with whomever I interact. This is the process of our self-realization, whichever of the four discussed yoga methods we choose. K's teaching and approach to dissolving our conditioning via our self-awareness would make him a Jnana yogi.

I noticed that when I fully understood something, anything, I became free of it. It left no residue of thought in me. There was no accumulation in my collective conditioning then. The more aware I stayed, the more my understanding grew of myself and my behavior.

The question that I asked myself was, *Can I stay equanimous irrespective of my circumstances, knowing full well that I cannot, in most cases, control my circumstances?*

I also noticed that I could not force myself for long to stay happy, joyous, kind, or compassionate on the surface. I noticed that as I kept dissolving my stored conditioning emotion by emotion as it arose, by watching each emotion choicelessly bubble up from deep in my psyche without giving the emotion new fuel, I was able to slightly lower its intensity each successive time. As I did so, the level of happiness, harmony, and peace I was naturally experiencing kept rising. I started being and staying happy for no reason. Even when difficult situations arose in my daily life, I was able to process them really fast, and each time took less time to get back to my new joyous steady state.

This exact same process is at work, undoubtedly with more intensity, because I had to stay quiet for nine long days at each of the ten-day Vipassana retreats (discussed in detail later in the book) I attended in 2013 and 2014. The experience of my internal self-purifying was simply more intense and penetrating then because my mind was not allowed to hide anywhere in my journaling, iPad, iPhone, human interactions and conversations, physical exercises, sex, drugs and alcohol, or even food. As all such props got taken away (these are the basic rules to be followed while there), I had no choice in my deep meditations but to look at the bubbling-up, deeply buried, and often seemingly long-forgotten emotions. I realized then that no hurt or grief or fear ever truly leaves us till we allow it by simply watching it without giving it more fuel and understanding it with full awareness.

I realized then that my primordial innate nature is that of love, peace, humbleness, and kindness and that all these attributes are waiting patiently within me (and each of us) to be simply discovered and realized. Everything I needed to experience in this state of my self-realization I came already equipped with. As Ramana Maharshi, Adi Shankara, K, and every true self-realized Jnana yogi reminds us, *we are that*.

In such a state of our self-realization or flowering, our love becomes nonpossessive and unconditional. Then when we love, we don't feel wounded when our love is not returned. Only such love is love.

Out of all the four yoga paths and their prominent examples I have discussed so far, Jnana yoga is the hardest to practice but the fastest to get us to our final victory. It does require a fully open, curious, investigative, and honest mind that can look at itself from all directions. The easiest is Bhakti yoga, which often takes the longest.

I also realized that my daily mental conflicts, irrespective of their source—for example someone cutting me off on the freeway—depleted my energy greatly. I have a limited amount of energy every day, so I have to be very cognizant of how or why I am depleting it. Right away this meant that I had to let go of relationships that were a source of such depletion on a daily basis. Additionally, I had to make sure I didn't leak my precious energy if someone tried to provoke me to do so in my daily interactions. As Gandhi had said so aptly, "Nobody can hurt me without my permission." As I became more mindful of all this, I started conserving my energy more and feeling better and staying happier longer. I felt I had control over myself. By such simple steps of staying fully aware of how and why I was acting as I was, I kept becoming and staying happier and harmonious longer and even in previously difficult situations. I was just letting stuff roll off and kept feeling less and less indignant when someone said something small or petty intentionally or unintentionally. This was my process of transcending my ego fully at work.

Ojai Trip, Summer 2011

I and Shelly decided to go visit Krishnamurti's Ojai headquarters, or his ashram. I wanted to see Pine Cottage, sit there, meditate, and experience the energy at the ashram. Pine Cottage is the name of the house where K lived for many years and also the place where he died. K traveled the world for over sixty years and gave public talks about the nature and experience of reality (what most call God) and man's functioning role in it.

We landed in Los Angeles, rented a car, and drove nearly two hours to get to Ojai. We decided to stay at the local Ojai Valley Inn and Spa rather than staying on the ashram premises. As we drove through town, I immediately liked the energy of the town. It was very laid back with cute little downtown shops and restaurants and seemingly happy people.

The next day, after our workout and breakfast, we stopped by the small office building toward the left that I saw on entering the property. The property is beautiful with orange groves stretching out far, followed by distant hills. I could just imagine K walking among the orange trees. Krishnamurti's love of nature and description of its subtleties is unparalleled in modern times I think. His last book, *Krishnamurti to Himself: His Last Journal*, was produced from his own personal dictation into a tape recorder during his final years when his hand became too shaky and he could not write anymore. Along with *Krishnamurti's Notebook*, these two books in my mind are a testimony to the vastness of the man and his work. If you allow him, K can clean you up and purify you from within completely—he is that intense. At least that is the effect he had on me as I dove deeper into him, or I should say, as he sucked me in.

Often our own built-in fears and apprehensions come in the way of our naked watching of ourselves. Once we stop pointing fingers at people as being the chief cause of our grief and problems, the next stage shows up when we can start pointing that finger at ourselves each time, to see what within us needs to be looked at and healed. This naked, choiceless self-observation is essential if we are to dissolve and transcend our ego, so as to dissolve our ignorance. It is hard work for most of us, but essential. Often it brings up old wounds still not healed. Because of our imaginary fears, we keep the wounds covered, thinking time will heal them, but each time, we are made to realize as they keep flaring up that time does not heal—it merely numbs.

Every wound, grief, fear, or hurt has to be understood for it to self-heal and thus dissolve. Once it self-heals via our choiceless self-observation, we release it from our accumulated conditioning. This process has to go on till we completely empty ourselves of our conditioning. The evidence that we are doing so is the gradual but unmistakable sense of joy, happiness, and perpetual peace that takes over us, arising from within us automatically. No effort needs to be made to uncork this boundless bottled-up unconditional love from within each of us. This is its primordial nature. All we have to do is burn our conditioning that is masking it. It is there waiting patiently to be experienced. In my own direct experience, the taste of this sweet water within each of us is our union with God as love.

This is the proof that our hard work and internal digging is working and self-healing and wholeness within is indeed returning. I (and so many others) can personally attest to the successful working of this mechanism. We each are made the same way within. What is sacred in me is also sacred in you, dear reader. If we continue on with this self-purification process, eventually our state of Nirvikalpa Samadhi or self-realization is experienced. It is the state of complete equanimity and bliss that never leaves us. This is who we are. Each one of us. We are that.

The other interesting thing I will add here from my own direct experience of this mechanism at work within each of us is that once sufficient internal self-cleaning or scrubbing has occurred via our meditations and self-awareness work, the pull of this God intoxication within becomes so strong and irresistible that the remaining process or work of self-cleaning kicks into high gear all by itself. All I had to do was simply get out of my own way and let the process take over. This presence of God within, love within, each of us is present in equal measure, simply waiting to be experienced by each of us through our own self digging. Religion, belief in a certain version of God, has no bearing on this experience. As long as we are human, we are entitled to this experience of self-realization, our oneness with our higher self within. In fact, this is the only reason we take birth in each incarnation, to get ever so closer each time via our work of self-purification.

As we walked toward the Pine Cottage, K's home of so many years, I saw that the pepper tree under which K had his acutely physical and very painful experience of transformation when he was all of twenty-eight in 1922 was still there. This experience, which K called "the Process," has been discussed at length in many of his earlier books by his biographers, Mary Lutyens and Pupul Jayakar, among others. I also noticed that there were still the two statues of the Nandi bull, the sacred bull revered in the South of India, which is supposed to have served as the mount of Lord Shiva. On receiving the crates with these two bulls from a well-wisher of his in India, Krishnamurti himself is said to have performed the sacred washing of the bulls with milk before placing them facing as exactly prescribed by custom in India.

We walked through the red front door into the cottage. There weren't any other visitors at that time luckily. Shelly knew well how much of an impact K had on my transformation by then, so she left me alone to go further inside. I always loved that about her. She knew when to leave me alone. With permission from the staff at hand, I headed first toward his bedroom on the right-hand side and through there to the living-room area, via a door to the right of the room, that he shared with Mary Zimbalist, who had an adjoining bedroom to his on the other side. There was a red-cushioned simple wooden sofa, if I recall correctly, by one side of the wall. The room was utterly quiet. I felt a palpable sense that something was going to happen. I could almost feel K's energy still there. By then I had not only read but also seen a live demonstration of psychometry from the medium I saw in San Francisco whom I mention at the start of my book. He, while holding my car keys during the one-hour session, told me point-blank that he saw a yellow car that I owned, which, by the way, was parked two blocks from his apartment on the third floor, where we were sitting. I had not mentioned anything about my car, much less its color, to the medium Felix. So I knew firsthand that objects retained the memory or energy of people who came in contact with them.

I sat down and closed my eyes in anticipation. Soon I could feel this energy take over me, and it made me almost light-headed. It's purity and its effect on me was different from what I had experienced till then. I remember being there for about an hour, and I came out feeling cleaner and purer. Usually, whenever I have an intense meditative experience, its effects show up in the form of tears of happiness, joy, and connection that start rolling down my cheeks. I had no tears this time. The experience felt like I was part of a void, an emptiness that had no attributes, no emotion. Before leaving, I remember writing an entry in the logbook, adding that it was a really intense meditative experience.

On coming outside, the sun was fully up, and we walked around and took the place in. We walked to the adjacent property called Arya Vihara, which is now a guest house. I remember seeing a Japanese guy on the front lawn, doing aikido with an invisible opponent. He looked really cool. From there we headed to the office of the ashram one more time. I wanted to get a photo of K for my altar, knowing full well that while alive, he was not a fan of such adoration. I honestly didn't care. The reason to have him and others already on my altar was less to worship them and more to thank them for their help along my journey. Each person on my altar was someone I had deeply learned from and who had touched my heart. Growing up in India, this was to me the right and natural way to thank my teachers. I, thus, didn't see any issue with having K on my growing altar.

You Are Love

I had been supporting the Krishnamurti Foundation of America (KFA) organization financially, and I had talked to some of the staff there that day before. They showed us around the office. We also went to the strong room enclosed within the office building that contained all the originals of K's writings and speeches. I thought that was pretty cool. I inquired about a photo of K that I could use for my altar, and they smiled and said that K made sure no photos of him would be floating around for any such purpose. I thanked them, and we left.

On returning back home, a couple of days later, in the mail, I received a used copy of his beautiful photo book, *One Thousand Moons: Krishnamurti at Eighty-Five,* done by Asit Chandmal, nephew of Pupul Jayakar, who wrote a mesmerizing biography of K. Unfortunately, I couldn't find any suitable photograph I liked in there either. Then I remembered I had read a book of his, *Meditations,* which had a photo of him on the cover I really liked. I found the book in my library, cut his photo from the cover, and put it in a small frame, and that's how K became part of my altar.

The next day, we drove around town and saw other properties affiliated with him, including the Oak Grove school, which he had started in Ojai. I also placed a call that evening expressing my desire to meet with Radha Sloss, who also lived in town, whose book I had read that detailed K's long affair with her mom, Rosalind. I just thought it would be good to talk with her to understand

K better. She graciously declined, adding that everything she wanted to say was in the book. I understood.

During those times when I was really high on K fever, a friend asked me if I thought that K appeared conflicting because of his long-standing affair with Rosalind. I laughed and said, "Thank God he was human."

CHAPTER 17

First Vipassana Visit, Kelseyville
(June 13–24, 2012)

BEFORE I START with my first Vipassana-course visit experience, I just want to mention that in March 2012, I changed the nameplate on my yellow Toyota FJ Cruiser from the generic I had before to BE PREM (be love). As I mentioned earlier, *prem* means divine or unconditional love in Hindi. Clearly, by early 2012, I had opened enough of my heart that I was not only feeling the unity of all humanity (we are all one) in my heart, but also the unconditional love that connected each of us as our essence within at our root level, and I felt the need to express it outwardly. Clearly, someone in California was ahead of me and had already taken the nameplate BE LOVE, so I settled for its Indian version, BE PREM.

How did I learn about the ten-day Vipassana meditation course? I was doing my yoga asanas that I do almost daily each morning in the stretch area at the Bay Club, and I started talking to this gal sitting next to me, stretching. There seemed to be a lot of talking going on around us, and I think I made a comment that it would be nice to be in a quiet zone for a while. She looked at me and asked if I had done the ten-day Vipassana course, and I said no. She then told me how she had done, if I recall, three of these courses and they had helped her immensely to get centered within. That's all I had to hear. I got back home, checked online to see what it was all about, was surprised to see that it was free, liked it, and ended up enrolling for a class three months out, figuring that would give me enough time to quit my cigar-smoking habit since smoking was absolutely not allowed there.

I had started smoking cigarettes in my final year of engineering at college. I remember those first cigarettes were just disgusting. I'm not sure why I got started. I think because a couple of my other friends used to smoke. Nobody pushed me though. Soon the nicotine got me hooked, and I was smoking maybe eight to ten cigarettes a day. This continued till I was working in Silicon Valley. It was 1990, and I was working as a product marketing engineer at Xicor Inc. in Milpitas. It started feeling odd standing outside smoking at the back of the building, so I decided to quit. That didn't last too long. I tried the patch then. That worked off and on. Then I came upon the brilliant idea to switch to smoking cigars. This way, at least, I wouldn't have to stand outside and look silly, and I would still be able to nurse my nicotine dependency. Plus, it was cool to be smoking cigars. By the time I moved to Atmel as a marketing manager in San Jose, I appeared clean as a whistle. I would go home and smoke half a cigar a day in the evening, and that's it. I would never feel the urge to smoke during the day. This setup continued for nearly nineteen years, till I was soon to go for my first Vipassana course. During this time, I had really enjoyed smoking all kinds of cigars, lots of Cubans included.

Once I seriously put my intention out, I simply stopped smoking about a month before the start of my class on June 13, 2012. It was a full ten-day course that was to finish on June 24 in the morning. We were supposed to get there by late afternoon on June 13. I chose, for this first course, the Vipassana center closer to where I lived, in Kelseyville, about an hour and a half away, in the mountains. I started early and got there around noon and hung around and familiarized myself with the place. We were served a light dinner early that evening after check-in and orientation. The course would officially start first thing the following day.

As a background, Vipassana, which means "seeing things as they really are," is an ancient Indian and, once Buddha revived it again long ago, now Buddhist way of self-discovery and purification via our meditative efforts. It is completely nonsectarian.

S. N. Goenka, who passed away in 2013 at the age of eighty-nine, was a Burmese-born Indian businessman. According to him, becoming very rich at an early age made him full of himself, and he looked at people who had less as inferior. He had a large ego that constantly needed to be fed, which made him very unhappy and un-satisfied with himself no matter how much he had or did. This resulted in big migraine headaches that would not go away. Also, he was, according to himself, a very angry man. He tried the usual Indian methods he knew of, such as Bhakti yoga or chanting and mantra singing in front of a deity, with minimal results. He also tried to study his scriptures with minimal lasting benefit. According to him, none of these went deep enough to bring about lasting change in his behavior. Then he heard about a wise man by the name of Sayagyi U Ba Khin, and he became his teacher in Burma. His teacher used to teach this ten-day Vipassana course that the Buddha is also said to have taught his disciples. Goenka quotes his master as saying that his habits lie deep in his subconscious and not at the surface level, and thus they cannot be eradicated through devotional chanting and mantra singing only.

Fast-forward, Goenka loved the course, became a fan, sold his business in Burma, and moved to India in 1969 to start teaching this ancient Indian methodology of self-purification at his first center in Bombay. From those humble beginnings, there are now over 225 Vipassana centers worldwide in over ninety-four countries training one hundred twenty thousand students in this technique of self-purification through self-awareness every year. The best part is that the whole ten-day course is completely free. Each center is run as a nonprofit, and old students, those who take a course there, on realizing the tremendous personal benefit start supporting it. There is a lot of volunteer work for cooking, cleaning, and general upkeep of each facility, which is taken care of within the local community. It's a great model in self-sufficiency, and this ancient technique really works. Many organizations have tried to copy this model in a three-, five-, or seven-day course with partial talking; no talking allowed, but there is something about the human mind and its need of self-purification that wants to take ten days. Somehow we are not able to go deep within during shorter durations, and so the self-purification work is never fully complete. Goenka knew this from his own such experiments early on—thus his insistence on ten full days.

There were some other basic rules I had to sign up for before being allowed to take the course. There is no conversation allowed during the first full nine days, and even making eye contact is discouraged. No personal food can be taken with you. Men and women are housed in separate dorms and have separate eating areas and are purposely kept separate the whole time. I could not take my phone in with me to my dorm, and no iPad, journaling, or reading any book of any kind. No exercise was allowed except gentle walking on preprescribed pathways on the property. There was no lying, cheating, stealing, sex, alcohol, or drugs of any kind except medications.

We were to get up at four every morning. Breakfast was from six thirty to eight. There was a one-hour lunch break at eleven and a very light dinner of a piece of fruit and a cup of tea at five. In between meals, there were about nine to ten hours of daily meditations with about half of them being compulsory group-meditation sessions in the dhamma hall that I had to show up for, and the other half I could either do in my room or go to the hall. I had never meditated so much in a day. I also was kind of scared to not get enough food to eat during the day, especially at dinnertime. What the heck; I wanted to do this thing. Bedtime was nine thirty each night.

I recall we had about sixty students split evenly between males and females. I was later to understand fully the great benefit of not being allowed to bring any food or other items that could end up serving as props where my mind would want to hide during the course. By taking all of my mind's usual hiding places away—no phone or books, no chatting, no looking at the opposite sex, no computer, and no exercises—this meant that I had no choice but to look at the contents of my mind all day: my fears, anxiety, likes and dislikes, and their source. Looking at all this was the real purpose of this course. I also came to understand that my habits were constantly being shaped, without my conscious knowing, by all these unresolved old memories and emotions stuck deep within me, some from childhood or even from previous lives, who knows. All this unprocessed stuff gave form to my daily habits. If I couldn't go deep enough in my meditations to access and thaw this stuff, I would not really be able to bring about any meaningful self-transformation. This is why taking endless yoga re-treats or vacations couldn't really help me break my neg-ative habits all these years. This I fully understood from my own self-purification and direct experience after tak-ing my first Vipassana course.

During my meditations, by focusing my mind's full at-tention on my incoming and outgoing breath touching any small surface at the entrance of my nostrils, helped me disengage my active conscious mind of other incom-ing conscious thoughts such that these deeply buried emotions had the space to bubble up and come into my mind's full conscious view. This is why chatting was not al-lowed at all in the course, so that my mind could have the opportunity to quiet its own activity. If my conscious mind could not quiet, all these deeply buried mental defile-ments of mine—my fears, jealously, anger, hatred, and so on—had no opportunity to bubble up for my active view-ing. This is why I had heard that people get nightmares when they are asleep, because the conscious mind is also at rest, and these deeply buried negative emotions get a chance to show up, some as nightmares. Now I under-stood why Goenka used to call this process so scientific and nonsectarian. It has nothing to do with any religion. All I had to do as a human being was to watch the con-tents of my mind and realize its ever-changing nature, and by this simple choiceless watching and understanding, I was able to start dissolving my stuff and keep lightening my load within.

In my daily meditations, different types of sensations kept showing up constantly on different parts of my body. This is the ever-changing nature of our sensational world that we live in and experience via our body and mind. The key is to always stay equanimous. By not reacting to such ever-changing bodily sensations, by simply watching and waiting for them to go away (and start in another area of my body soon), I was able to transcend them each time. Just don't react to the ever-changing nature of our reality. This was the basic message I was made to learn over and over again for nine full days. It got really hard some days, especially Goenka's monotonous and very repetitive voice and commands on the tapes that were being played at each of these dhamma-hall meditation sessions. There was one head teacher and one under him training I guess. The head teacher would walk in at the start of the session, put in the required tape for each meditation, and sit with us the entire time. I remember he reminded me a couple of times to pull down my shorts so they would be covering my knees, a requirement for guys wearing shorts.

Some people chose to sit on the floor, some with their mile-high cushions hid neatly under their draped shawls. I chose a chair, though I could have also sat on the floor. My goal was to focus more on my meditations and to worry less about my posture and its resulting pain and how to keep managing that the entire time.

This process is not easy of course. And this is why the insistence to stay the whole ten days—this was another rule they had. They knew from teaching these courses for so many years that if I could just hang in there and keep working through my stuff every day, I would eventually, by the end, feel much lighter, freer, and thus happier. This was exactly my experience and that of so many others. People were crying—letting out old, crusty, bad stuff that had been hiding in them for years and conditioning their perception of the world and of themselves. The whole experience was very cathartic for so many.

One of the most important techniques I learned to break my habits was to stop reacting to daily incoming stuff. Most of my incoming stuff showed up uninvited anyway, so I had to consciously learn to stop negatively reacting to it to maintain my daily equanimity. My equanimity was my jewel. I would not let anyone take it away from me, no matter what. If I didn't react and give in, nobody could steal my equanimity from me.

I also realized that often I was like a pendulum, swinging on a daily basis between the two extremes of loving something and hating something else. My human mind would habitually keep reacting to each of those two extreme emotional states in different ways and thus exhaust itself daily of its precious and limited energy. I was never aware of this behavior of my mind. Of course, new stuff would keep showing up daily that I was constantly loving or hating. Often what I ended up loving one day, I would change my mind and start disliking it many days later. The whole thing was a circus, and my mind was caught in it without even being aware of it. The goal of all this Vipassana work was to let my mental pendulum come to rest in the middle, to become equanimous, to stop reacting, irrespective of either extreme my mind was encountering. This was the way to my enduring happiness.

The food was really good and prepared by old students who were also sitting with us in the dhamma hall. Being a new student, I was to share my small room with another inmate, which was kind of difficult, but we both made it work. Bathrooms and shower were communal for each dorm and were kept clean by each of us taking turns to wipe and clean them every couple of days. The scene on my first couple of days reminded me of being in a mental asylum with so many inmates walking around dazed and avoiding each other's glances. I also realized, once the course started, that they had closed the main gates, so I couldn't even leave if I wanted to. My car was parked inside. I learned later of this new rule since sometimes students couldn't handle it and would leave at night and later regret it and try to re-enroll for a new course, thus wasting their and the organization's time and resources. From experience of doing so many courses every year, the two teachers also knew that if I could just get through days two and six, I would be home free. So their goal was to get me through the program in spite of myself because in the end they knew I would love it, which I truly did.

I recall a lot opening up for me during my first Vipassana course as I kept cleaning myself within. I opened my sixth and seventh chakras. I could in my meditations feel this intense tingling energy sensation moving and opening my chakras on very specific and defined meridian lines under my skin. It was amazing. There were times when my whole forehead, the area around my eyes, and my crown area at the top of my head was ablaze with tingling and pulsating activity. I could actually feel this intense energy coursing through my whole body, circling my two palm chakras. It was really cool. I knew I was being opened up from deep within. I think one night I did some astral travel as well. There was a forest area in front of our premises on the other side of the road, and I remember floating above the treetops, looking at everything under me as I was flying. The best part of the experience was the last full day (June 23) when we were allowed to talk after nine full days of complete silence. It was a riot. We formed a really close bond with each other.

By the last day (June 24), as we finished the meta meditation, blessing ourselves and the whole world to be peaceful, kind, and happy, voiced so sweetly by Goenka on tape, I started crying. I felt such love for being alive. Sitting that early morning in my preassigned seat, number nine on my plastic white chair, in the now very familiar dhamma hall, I became overwhelmed by the deep sense of my happiness and gratefulness for being guided to come here and to participate in this amazing course. What a blessing it was. I couldn't thank my spirit guides enough, who were watching over me constantly and guiding me on my journey. I also realized that I had also worked through Goenka's voice mental block I had felt early on.

On arriving back home, I realized that I had also lost four pounds, which was a side benefit. I remember my dad always reminding me to get on the right track in life, and then everything good starts happening by itself. I had quit smoking, had started losing weight, and was feeling so much more centered and happy. I was so impressed by the results of my course that I started to financially support the center, which I continued to do for some time so new students could have the same opportunity I did. I also ended up buying many of Goenka's books and meditation tapes from a shop not far from the main premises so I could keep up with the practice of daily one-hour meditations at home, which I did for a while.

CHAPTER 18

Taoists

WHAT DOES ONE call that state of mind that is completely empty of everything, abiding in its natural state of nothingness, in harmony with everything and everyone? Whatever thought is registered in the brain is immediately processed and the appropriate action taken, and having done its intended work, that thought simply vacates the brain without leaving any residue whatsoever. No accumulation of any kind of conditioning. Such a pristine, unencumbered state of mind is what Lao Tzu encourages us to achieve in our daily living through his writings.

Before he died, he is said to have written eighty-one sayings or poems, comprising of a total of about five thousand words, that capture the essence of what is today called Taoism. The book called the *Tao Te Ching* has survived for over twenty-five hundred years by now. This speaks to the depth of the universal wisdom left behind by Lao Tzu. The immediate attraction for me to Taoism, when I went deeper into Lao Tzu and then Chuang Tzu, was in the utter simplicity and freedom of the Way (Tao). Taoism is completely free of any and all rituals, dogma, or belief systems. It is simply carefree and natural living in complete freedom. While Confucius, like India's ancient Manu, left behind many written rules and laws for daily conduct, Lao Tzu's work is oriented around the spiritual refinement and eventual release from all bondage of a being. It shows how a human being can live his or her life in the present with full spontaneity and freedom.

As I read more of Lao and Chuang Tzu, I realized that when I got started on my path, in the initial years, my human mind was always trying to accept this and reject that, always seemingly caught in the opposites, comparing, selecting, choosing, and living in constant self-created duality.

What if I started receiving life with gratitude just as it was unfolding in front of me daily? If I liked someone, I did my part to catch their attention and interest. If they became interested as well, great. But if they didn't care to reciprocate my interest, could I, with love and humility and graciousness, let what happened between us simply pass? And when I encountered the person again the next day, could I simply smile even after that person had rejected me for whatever reason as if I was just meeting them for the first time? Initially on my journey, this hypothetical scenario would have been hard for me to bring to such a conclusion. But as I was getting deeper into Taoism, I realized I was already there.

The work that gets us "there" is, of course, our capacity of transcending our egos. Our egos as I mentioned earlier are simply our accumulated thoughts. Once understood, they stop bothering us in our minds and get to course in and out unhindered. Then there is no Velcro in our minds. This is our primordial natural state.

The more we are free of ourselves, the easier all this becomes. Then I can live in full equanimity whatever the scenario and its resultant conclusion. Nobody to hate, nothing to fear. Then there is the opportunity to start dancing with life on a daily basis, irrespective of its inevitable ups and downs. What is my ego, my *I*, but my condensed ignorance, my accumulated past? Once I understood who or what I was, it became so much easier to transcend myself and my thinking process. Then I just became a watcher, a witness, of my life's daily drama without getting stained by it. This is pure living, living the Tao.

The Tao is simply about living in the middle, not going or trying to stay at extremes, living in balance and harmony with the way things are. As they change, you adapt and change, remaining fully present. That good and bad are two sides of the same coin. We need bad to appreciate what good is. If everyone was beautiful, what would beauty mean?

Spontaneity is a sign of an empty mind, an unburdened mind, a mind that gets to process life's incoming drama fast. I realized as I was becoming happier from within, I was also becoming more spontaneous. I didn't have to try to be spontaneous; I just was. I realized all I really had to do was focus on my efforts of self-purification to keep cleaning my conditioning from within. All the good stuff then kept showing up effortlessly within.

As I purified and cleaned myself more, I realized I was not a Hindu but a human being first, whose beingness was this unconditional love that was welling up more and more within me daily. This love was impersonal, was not possessive, and was unconditional toward one and all. I stopped seeing people as black or white, gay or straight, Jews or Muslims, but as love. If someone did something mean to me, I would laugh it off and move on, knowing that the person was not a bad person but was simply ignorant still, as I probably was as well at some point during my own conscious evolution.

It became much easier for me to say to people I didn't know, "I love you."

CHAPTER 19

First John of God Visit

(April 13-27, 2013)

I REMEMBER INITIALLY learning about John of God (JOG) from Sheri. She had visited the Casa (his spiritual center in Abadiania, Brazil) many years ago. We met at a local restaurant in Mill Valley in early December 2012. Sheri brought along some cool-looking crystals of different colors and shapes she had bought at the Casa as well as a few books. I wrote down the names of the books. There was a book written by Heather Cumming and Karen Leffler about John of God and another book about another gentleman by the name of Chico Xavier, a Brazilian automatic writer. I didn't know then what an automatic writer was or did. Sheri also gave me Heather's website address and the name of the tour company, based in Stamford, Connecticut, that she had used. She also mentioned that it would be a very good idea to go as part of a tour on my first visit because most people only spoke Portuguese at the Casa, and having Heather as a translator was recommended, especially in conversing with the incorporated JOG. I remember being very excited about this new door opening for me, and I thanked Sheri for all her help. A year later I was also to buy those crystals from her for my altar as I had started doing healing work by then.

On getting home, I looked up the Amazon reviews on Heather and Karen's book and ordered it. I figured I'd wait on researching Chico Xavier. I also went online and started looking at potential dates for my trip. Each of these trips was of a two-week duration and was going to cost me $1,800 plus an extra charge if I wanted a single room, which I did. This would cover my stay, three meals a day, and all the help, guidance, and interface with the Casa while I was there. I had to buy my own airfare. I thought it was a good deal. The first available slot I could find was the trip I went on. It so happened that I ended up also celebrating my birthday (April 24) there. I thought that was meant to be and really pretty cool.

As an aside, I had also by now become very aware of my physical weight and wanted to look at ways of reducing it. At the start of April 2013, I had got a free body scan done at the Bay Club, which clocked my weight at 185.2 pounds and showed that I was 15 pounds' overweight.

I got all the arrangements figured out with Barbara in Stamford, got my Brazilian visa, and was ready well before time. I flew via Miami and from there a direct flight to Brasilia. This trip had about thirty Americans, and we were asked to meet and stay at a hotel in Brasilia. The next morning, Heather came with two big vans, and we hauled our bags into the vans and were ready for our trip to Abadiania, a small village about two hours from Brasilia. All of us were excited in the van. We were truly on a unique adventure of potential deep travels within each of us.

As we started to head out, we were told that we would be visiting some local monuments in Brasilia, including a church, and partaking in a delicious lunch. Brazil is God country, and Jesus is the king. The church we saw blew me away. I had never been to such a beautiful church before. As I sat down in one of the first pews, I loved how the sunlight was beating down on the different shades of blue stained-glass windows, bringing them softly aglow. I noticed there were also a couple of vertical columns with beautiful shades of pink in the stained glass. With this as a backdrop, I had in front of me a large, quiet, and beautiful figure of Christ on a cross. The soft glows of blue and pink light made the figure of Christ feel solemn and quietly very penetrating to me. The effect was mesmerizing. I closed my eyes in meditation and sat for a bit. This was the church of Dom Bosco.

Before leaving, I took a bunch of pictures as did everyone else. I did not know then that by the time this trip would be over, in two weeks, Jesus, Saint Ignatius, Prophet Solomon, Saint Francis Xavier, Dr. Augusto, and other beings of light at the Casa would open new doors of perception and unconditional love within me to take me in deeper.

Later that year, I was to acquaint myself with a fine painter whose works I would see in an art auction in San Francisco. I would then hire the painter to make me not only a beautiful painting of this church but many others. All this excitement, adventure, and learning was in front of me. I just had to stay open and keep going where I was being led.

On getting to Rei Davi, the hotel we were staying at, I saw photos of Heather having facilitated Oprah Winfrey's visit to JOG. I thought it was really cool of Oprah, such a big celebrity, to have such an open mind to want to come and investigate what was going on in this small village in Central Brazil.

We were very excited, and after getting our assigned rooms, freshening up, and changing into white clothes, we took off on foot to see the main attraction. It is strongly recommended to wear white on days that JOG is present—Wednesday, Thursday, and Friday—but I saw that many in my group were already in their whites. I was told the reason for wearing white is that it is easier for the entities who incorporate through JOG to see us more clearly and fully.

The Casa was under a ten-minute walk. It was warm already in Brazil, about eighty degrees. Upon entering the premises, I and some others made our way to the main hall with many people already sitting there on chairs with their eyes closed. I sat down on one of the chairs and saw that people, one by one, would go up to a triangle on the big wall facing me—which had large photos of Jesus, Mary, St. Ignatius, and other mostly Christian saints—and bow their heads into a rather large triangle hung on the wall, and sometimes they would also leave letters or photos of their loved ones. I just sat there and watched. I also noticed some people in wheelchairs, one on a crutch, and some not looking 100 percent well. My real purpose of this visit was to investigate, see, and directly experience for myself what was going on here at the Casa in the work of JOG. Luckily, I was physically healthy as far I could tell. But I realized that many people were there for physical healings as well, not just emotional and spiritual healing like myself.

I made my way out of the main hall and walked around the rest of the small compound of various buildings. I sat in the garden for a while and generally took the place in. I saw a painting of a being of light on the outside backside of the main hall where I had sat earlier, which I found intriguing. I sat in front of it for a bit and left.

I spent the next day, Tuesday, getting organized. We were given details about the workings of the Casa, the protocol once there, and other necessary details for our first big day, which was Wednesday morning.

I got up early the next day, and we all met downstairs in the lobby, finished our breakfast, and headed to the Casa. I felt a lot of excitement as we were getting there.

Long lines had already started forming, and the main hall was getting fuller. There had to have been over five hundred people there already, and the day was just getting started. When my turn came, I rose from my seat, walked a bit, and became part of the standing line waiting to go into the first current room. As I entered the first current (meditation) room, there were people already sitting on parallel wooden benches in deep meditation. I noticed the various Christian saints and their photos hanging on the walls as I was walking through the rooms, single file in line. The music playing through the speakers was in Portuguese and sounded very beautiful and heartfelt to me. JOG was already incorporated and sitting on his chair facing us, and one by one, we walked to and past him. In the brief time I was to be in front of him, he would look at me like an energy entity that I am on a subatomic level, see what kind of healing I needed, and relay that to Heather, who would be standing right next to us. I could also ask any question or relay any problem or issue I wanted, again through Heather to him. That was the general protocol. I saw huge crystals stationed around him, the size of which I would have a hard time putting my arms around. I was told the goal of all these crystals and all the people sitting in meditations in the three connected but different rooms was to hold up the current or energy that was there so JOG could stay incorporated and the entities, through him, could keep doing the required healing work. On the three days every week that JOG was there, often over a thousand people would show up unannounced from all over the world, including many from Brazil. This would keep JOG occupied late into the day.

When my turn came to be in front of the entity, I asked the entity the question of my desire to further open my spiritual path deeper and wider. The entity said he would and told me to get a crystal bed session along with the Casa herbs. I went to the store, paid the ten dollars and secured my half-hour crystal bed session for later that afternoon. I also started on one of many bottles of herbal capsules that are to be bought at the Casa pharmacy on the written instruction of the incorporated JOG. These sales and sales at the book store are how the Casa stays operational. There is no charge to see JOG or for the soup that is dispensed free every day when JOG incorporates there. I also was curious and later asked Heather who the incorporating entity was when I was in front of JOG. She mentioned Dr. Augusto.

Later in the afternoon, I went for my crystal bed session, which was really an amazing experience. On entering the small room and lying down on a makeshift bed, I saw myself under a simple plastic apparatus that had seven small arms sticking out, holding different (electric lighted) colored crystals at their ends positioned on my body where my invisible energetic chakras are supposed to be. I was encountering ancient India again, this time in Brazil. I noticed that the different colored-glass crystals on each stem corresponded with the color of each chakra that the ancient Indian yogis had discovered over thirty-five hundred years ago in their deep meditations. The basic idea in my crystal bed session was to physically try to further activate my different energetic chakras by throwing a similar external light on them to their inherent color. Often when our bodies get diseased with too much self-inflicted stress, such that we start forming heavy energetic blocks within us, which end up blocking and impeding the flow of universal energy (prana or chi) through us, such a methodology makes them dissolve. By the time I was done on that trip, I had at least six or seven such sessions. During each session, I would go very deep within myself as the speaker in the room played soft melodious local Portuguese Christian songs.

Our physical bodies have, invisible to most eyes, a corresponding energetic component. It primarily comprises of seven chakras or spinning vortices with connecting meridian lines (nadis) throughout our body. It is through this energetic apparatus that universal energy keeps getting absorbed in us to self-heal and keep our physical bodies in prime health. Our daily stress if not skillfully dissolved via our meditations and other mindful practices get to form energetic blocks that over time manifest as physical disease. Our chakras get to slow down or often stop spinning when this happens. Then they stop absorbing the life-force energy all around us. The primary purpose of crystal bed sessions or other healings modalities that one encounters are simply to get our chakras spinning again.

Psychic mediums are able to see this energetic body of ours and our energetic blocks.

It was my third active day, I remember, Friday, when I truly first connected with the energy at the Casa. Another way to say this would be when that energy at the Casa started to open me up from within. This was also my deep desire I had relayed to the entity Dr. Augusto two days prior. I had elected to sit in meditation that morning. I had never meditated for multiple hours before I got to the Casa, and this becomes a sort of requirement if one elects to sit and hold current in one of the three rooms. I bravely elected to stand in the line that started seating participants in one of the three meditation rooms starting about seven in the morning, if I recall correctly. Often one is supposed to sit during the entire session till JOG finishes and breaks for lunch. I figured I would try it now that I was there.

Soon after we were seated, we were asked to close our eyes as a lady very beautifully started saying a local Christian prayer. Her voice just tugged at my heart that morning. Soon, I started to feel a tingling sensation on my arms and hands, especially on my palms. Then it began on my forehead. I realized this was the same tingling feeling I had started to experience at my Vipassana course last year. It just felt much more intense here. I remember thinking it was really cool—whatever was here was definitely potent and palpable for me. Pretty soon I was feeling like someone was trying to poke me with small needles all over my forehead; on top of my head; and along my arms, hands, palms, and practically all over my body. I also started feeling like I couldn't move even if I tried and that I was in the grip of an energetic field present there. It just took me in. This is probably the best way to describe this encounter. I soon had tears rolling down my cheeks. I was so overwhelmed by this energy that I folded my hands in the air in front of me and thanked this energy and love that was working through me. I lasted like this for less than two hours and felt I had had enough. I opened my eyes, flagged a helper, and left. I walked into the morning sun in a daze. I found a bench to sit on. It was empty, so I lay on it for a while, feeling the soothing heat of the sun on my face and body. No two spiritual experiences are the same. Each time, we encounter new depth within us.

Lying where I was, as I turned to my side, I could see from far away that same photo I had seen many times while at the Casa—this being of light staring back. I had tried to sit in front of it like I saw many people doing and tried to meditate, but nothing would happen, and soon I'd leave each time.

That day, I found that photo very intriguing from afar, as if calling me. I immediately got up, walked closer to it, and sat down on a seat right in front of it. I now was maybe five feet from it. I noticed it was an old charcoal sketch, and the thin transparent plastic sheet that apparently covered the sketch was coming off on one of the side edges. And the frame had a faded red tone to it. I also noticed that I had sat in front of this photo a couple of times before but had failed to notice all of what I just did. This time, the more I looked at it, the more it pulled me in. I noticed the eyes of this figure were almost staring at me in a very penetrating way. Soon I couldn't keep my eyes open to these eyes staring back at me. I started feeling light-headed, and my eyes closed. I immediately got pulled into myself in a very deep meditation right away. Soon I had tears in my eyes again, a sign for me that I was deeply connected within myself with my higher self. I sat there for a while and almost had to force myself to open my eyes. I felt intoxicated. Who needed to drink alcohol or do drugs when one could partake of this pure nectar, I remember thinking later. Whatever energy was here, it was very palpable and extremely strong, and I was definitely experiencing it with full force now. I just had to surrender to the whole unfolding for the rest of the trip and let it guide me. I also asked some people about that photo of that being of light with very penetrating eyes. I was told he was Solomon, the great King Solomon of the Jews.

My first encounter with this charcoal sketch of Solomon was so intense that I was later to find and hire another good artist who would draw a very similar portrait charcoal sketch of Solomon for me for my home altar.

In hindsight I have come to realize that when one fully comes into the grip of this energy, there is nothing one can do; it cleanses, purifies, and guides you how it will. All I could do was let go and allow the process to unfold. And the deeper I went in my meditations the rest of my trip, the more intoxicated I felt each time. I was ecstatic. I knew a new way, and a deeper door of perception and awareness within me had been opened, just as I had requested.

I went in front of the entity two more times on that trip. Once, I encountered Saint Francis Xavier, and the other time, another entity, Jose Valdavino.

I also had a couple of spiritual operations for which I was supposed to rest in my room for at least twenty-four hours each time.

The Casa and the surrounding area around it is basically an intense energy vortex facilitated by the energy of the entities that work through JOG. The ground deep underneath also has a bed of crystals that helps keep this energy localized, charged, and centered and makes this energy experience that much stronger. It is probably much more than all this, but at the basic level, that is how I look at it. Anyone who comes in contact with this intense energy gets benefit, unasked. This is the innate nature of all the spirit entities that come through JOG at the Casa. This is the nature of spirit, to heal us unasked. The only thing I had to do while there was to keep an open mind and heart and to allow them to do their jobs.

I will give another example of the power and intensity of this energy that is available at the Casa. One morning we were all filed, as usual, by the wall at the corner side of the small stage in the main hall, waiting to be called as part of Heather's group to go in. On some days JOG would do a live and physical performance of his operations for all present to see. People would be clicking away and taking video. That day was no different. These physical operations can be the "nose job" or the "scraping of the eye" job. Sometimes he also cuts a small portion of skin on someone's chest to clean something out from within and simply sews the cut with a needle. All this is covered and shown very well in the movie *Healing* that is mentioned at the end of the book in the list of movies to see and which I highly recommend every reader watch. I have watched the movie now close to ten times. Simply by watching the movie, I can experience some healing effects of the Casa.

That morning as JOG stepped onto the stage to start his operation fully incorporated, this girl standing two feet from me almost fainted. One can see how slowly JOG starts to walk when he is incorporated, often needing someone to hold his hand and simply staring as he walks by. The intensity of the energy she was receiving from JOG, who was now standing less than five feet from us, coupled with probably the accumulated heaviness of her own mental and emotional blocks within took her down. They wheeled her off on a chair, and soon she was fine. The bigger point I am making here is that the nature of this energy is to clean us, and depending on our level of purification needed, it can and will take us down to do its job.

Often after getting invisible spiritual operations, we were to go back to the hotel and lie down and rest for at least a day. I would often not see people for days. The same process was at work. Depending on the purification needed, the energy was going to keep you down till it purified you enough. No wonder with every operation and passing day, we were all feeling that much happier, freer, connected with each other and ourselves, and more peaceful. I noticed we were all laughing and hugging more during our lunch and dinner sessions, like there was no care left in the world to worry about.

In hindsight this was the normal human self-purification process at work and its inevitable results. The less conditioning that is left within us, the happier, freer, and more spontaneous we feel, each one of us. We are all made the same way innately.

Unfortunately, if we don't change our daily habits after getting back from such trips, these energy blocks we just dissolved start to reaccumulate within us due to our daily encountered friction from living and existing in this world, and the same process now starts to accelerate in the other direction. This is why having a daily meditation practice is so essential. To me meditation is simply a tool I use to go within to keep me mentally and emotionally clean on a daily basis. Whatever energy blocks due to my daily stress get accumulated in me, I want to make sure I keep dissolving them as I go along. If not removed and dissolved on a timely basis, these energy blocks eventually manifest as physical disease in our bodies. Medical science tells us that.

One evening, on the weekend, we all went to the Casa waterfalls close-by. The water was refreshing and cold. One by one, we stood under it.

On April 24, my birthday, Heather was so sweet to remember it and made sure there was a big chocolate cake after dinner for all of us. We took photos, and I remember wearing a rosary that evening that I had bought from the Casa bookstore. By this time everything was the same to me—Hindu, Christian, Sufi, Jew, black or white, believer or unbeliever—all simply a manifestation of the one love.

She also gave me a small box with little pieces of emerald crystals that she had gotten from her close and long association with JOG. I still have all of them and treasure them. I still vividly remember my last day there. During the early morning, some of us were headed out around five o'clock from Rei Davi to catch an early flight. As we were starting to pack our luggage in the big van to head out, Heather was there to make sure all went well. I was really touched by that. I think everyone in our group had a wonderful time with Heather, and I highly recommend her as a tour guide for your Casa visit.

I also remember encountering two photos of Chico Xavier at the Casa, one in the small office there and one in the main hall on the left wall. In the latter JOG is hugging him.

All I was doing was staying curious and with an open mind and heart was willing to be guided. I also knew I was not special. This same phenomenon is at work with each of us. The key is to stay open-minded and to open the door when someone knocks.

I had brought with me, for my altar at home, two photos of Jesus, one of Saint Ignatius, one of Solomon (the only one available), one of Dr. Augusto, and a couple of Casa triangles. I also got all this stuff signed by the entity each time I stood in line during the second week. I was thinking ahead. Promptly on getting back home, I got all the photos framed, and these were new additions to my growing altar.

Unfortunately, on this trip I could not find a photo of Jose Valdavino or Saint Francis Xavier, the other two entities along with Dr. Augusto that came through for me. I had to find a way to thank them for their continued guidance on my amazing journey. This I got to resolve later when I got two paintings made of church altars dedicated to Saint Francis Xavier, and I also ended up finding a photo of Jose Valdavino at the Casa shop on my next trip, which I then added to my altar.

CHAPTER 20

Second Vipassana Visit, North Fork (August 7-18, 2013)

I HAD SUCH a positive first experience with Vipassana that I decided to do another course so I could clean myself even more within. This time I wanted to go to the other center in Northern California by Yosemite. It was a much larger center. Being an old student now and this being a bigger center, I was hoping to get my own room, which I did.

I also discovered on getting there that my dorm was air conditioned. Wow, so cool. The journey from my house was close to four hours. I knew the whole course now, so I was pretty relaxed. I was also excited about this particular center because they had recently completed building a brand new pagoda that sat right next to the large dhamma hall.

Our course probably had close to eighty participants and the same format of two teachers. Again, I chose to sit on a chair by the side of a wall so I could focus more on going within than having to worry about managing the pain in my legs as I went along.

By the second day into the course, I realized I didn't need to be there. My work of self-purification via Vipassana was done. I was clean within. Nothing negative was bubbling up from my unconscious into my conscious mind during my deeper meditations. I could have been meditating at home or there, one and the same thing. But I had to come the second time to know that I was done with it, that I had completed my work. My steady state by the time I had gone for this course was one of equanimity, perpetual happiness, and peace within and without. Whenever something in my daily life would challenge my steady state, I would simply find time to sit in meditation for a half hour and dissolve whatever I was holding within that was bothering me, and I was fresh again. This is why having a daily meditation practice is a must, to keep dissolving as we go along. This way we never give any conditioning (or friction) that we encounter via our daily living a chance to accumulate within, and we keep living life ever free and pure, dancing in the here and now. The whole thing was so simple to me.

A stage then comes in our daily living when we encounter no resistance or conflicts within. We start to fly and glide like the eagle in the sky, completely carefree. Everything we experience moves right through us without sticking because we understand the nature of non-reality. There is no Velcro left within. Then we automatically allow the attributes of our higher self to shine through us.

I tried to make the best of my visit. I really enjoyed the quieter meditations in my assigned cell in the pagoda. I would sit in full lotus and, slowly each day, I'd try to beat the prior day's time. I remember getting to over thirty-five minutes in full lotus position in my meditations without any use of a bolster or cushion, just on flat carpeted floor in the pagoda.

One of the things I really enjoyed during my first and second Vipassanas was Goenka's evening video sessions. He was hilarious and so awesome in his simple style of presentation. In spite of the long days, I think everyone looked forward to these evening sessions. I liked them so much I ended up buying the complete DVD set, and this set is listed in the videos to watch at the end of the book.

One of the basic messages I took away from the course each time was that if I don't stay equanimous in my daily living in spite of whatever is coming at me in terms of my evolving circumstances, which are often out of my control anyway, I will keep building new *sankharas,* or mental defilements. These new sankharas will cause me to keep generating new karma that has to be borne out by me in this and successive lives. To break this cycle, first I have to stop generating any new defilements by always staying equanimous to all incoming daily life stuff. The next step, via my daily meditations is, as old sankharas stored deep within my psyche keep bubbling up into my conscious mind, by choicelessly watching them without giving them any new fuel, I let them dissolve. This way, over time, I break my cycle of birth and death. My mental defilements are my anger, hatred, jealousy, envy, greed, and other such negative emotions.

Our world is a big classroom, and we come into each life with our handpicked drama and actors simply to dissolve our sankharas and hopefully not to generate many new ones. To make our world more peaceful and happier, we have to stop inflicting and passing on pain to others. We have to learn to break this cycle first.

Our daily life events are constantly changing (*anicca*). By doing our daily dharma, our necessary actions, but staying equanimous to all resultant developments, we stop generating new *sankharas*. This is the first and most important step to self-purification. Unless this is achieved, our process of self-purification cannot build. I have tested this through my own direct experience of living the past many years. It works. Staying equanimous is my treasure, my jewel—I have to hold on to it no matter what.

Vipassana meditation is simply a technique to examine my body part by part, piece by piece, to simply observe all the different sensations that arise to pass away. Arise to pass away. Nothing is permanent. Everything is *anicca, anicca*—changing, changing. So why should I react to an ever-changing situation? I need to stay focused on doing my dharma choicelessly and without any attachment to the results. This is also one of the basic messages of the *Gita.*

Another observation and learning that really helped me was to "keep moving" forward without holding on to my past. My past was dead. I learn from those experiences and let them go; otherwise, my past keeps slowing me down as excess baggage I need to keep lugging with me. By fully understanding that everything is constantly changing, I live in the present and let go of it as soon as it passes and becomes my past. This way I stay free, light, and in the present moment.

Since it is so important from my own direct experience, I will say this again. It is imperative to keep moving forward. Hold on to a guru, a sacred book, or a sacred place just as long as you need to fully understand and make it a part of you. As soon as that happens, you will automatically release it. If you do not, it means you are stuck. Find out why. Keep moving. Often we tend to drag our past into our present because of our fears and insecurities. Choicelessly watch your fear and insecurity, as emotions, arise in your daily living, and by not giving them any new fuel or energy, let them lessen their hold on you each time they show up. It's a very methodical and scientific method of self-observation that totally works.

If you are not moving, you are not making progress on your spiritual journey. Your spiritual journey is your life that you are living on a daily basis. That implies, if you're not moving, you are not living, just existing.

Eventually, the only book that needs to be read, fully understood, and mastered is ourselves. And that can only happen in relationships, not in isolation. And for that we have to keep moving, keep experiencing. That is the only purpose of each life, simply to experience it so as to complete our understanding of who we truly are, each one of us—divine beings made of love within. Each of us is made the same way. What is sacred in you is also sacred in me. This is the evolving process toward our self-realization in successive lives.

CHAPTER 21

Spiritism and Chico Xavier

I HEARD ABOUT Chico Xavier, the Brazilian automatic writer, as I researched other Brazilian psychics and mediums beyond John of God. I then also stumbled upon, and thoroughly enjoyed, researching Ze Arigo, a phenomenon I will discuss in the next chapter.

John of God, Chico, and Arigo, discussed in this book, are all Spiritists. Spiritism was a philosophy and religion started by Allan Kardec, a French educator, in 1857 when he researched, documented, codified, and published the first of many spirit-directed books whose contents were received through various anonymous mediums he knew. He himself was not a medium. Spiritists believe in the core original teachings of Jesus Christ before the development of churches and religious hierarchies.

Spiritualism is the belief that there is more to a human body than just material matter. The main difference between Spiritism and spiritualism is the absolute belief in karma and reincarnation for the Spiritist. Both also believe in the existence and communication with a spirit world to which one enters after physical bodily death.

All the work (psychic surgery) that John of God has been performing for over fifty years now would not have been possible without help from elevated and wise spirits in the spirit world, some of whom lived on earth in recent memory.

My interest grew in Spiritism as I saw the phenomenon of JOG live on my two-week trip to Abadiania. Spiritism also had, for me, some resemblance to Hinduism in its mutual belief in karma, reincarnation, and the existence of a spirit world as well as the belief in the eternal nature of our souls. Our souls come in each incarnation on earth with the primary purpose of learning and growing from their experiences and thus elevating themselves in God wisdom. I knew this to be common in both as well. Hindus called their God Brahman, while Spiritists called their God Jesus Christ. Spiritism is primarily based in Brazil.

If I truly wanted to figure out a coherent framework to the workings of my life—which was one of my goals when I started out in 2006—I had to stay open and research any and all phenomenon, however strange it initially looked to me. This is why I had gone to visit John of God in the first place. What was the message that these spirits were communicating to how I should be living my remaining life on earth? Did it sound right and logical to me? My end goal was to live the most perfect life I could for myself and for my remaining years. All I was researching was what it was and if there was a common theme to the message. *There should be if it was to be true and real,* I thought. I knew the basic experience and message of the yogis of *The Upanishads* and the *Gita* and that of the various self-realized beings of light already discussed so far. I had also read by now, in good detail, the basic message of love, peace, and brotherhood that Jesus exemplified via his life. I also knew about the basic message of love that the various NDErs (near-death experiencers) brought back for us of whatever little they were shown of the spirit realm. Everything sounded logical and made sense to me so far.

What about these spirits of Spiritism who were communicating from the spirit world through Chico, Arigo, as we will see later, and JOG?

Chico Xavier, who died in 2002 at the age of ninety-two, was an almost illiterate man who went to school only till fifth grade, dropping out then to work as a shop assistant. He realized early on that he was an automatic writer, where spirits would take control of him and his right hand and start moving it ferociously to write at a speed of about one page per minute. When he was in such a trance, he would cover his eyes with his left hand as his right would start writing on its own. A person sitting close-by and helping him would simply put a new sheet of paper where the now-completed old sheet was. His hand would never overreach the size of the paper. He wrote over 458 books in his lifetime and had already sold well over fifty million copies by the end of 2010. The royalties from his books support the over two thousand Spiritist centers all over Brazil, which house needy children and adults. He did all this while he simply supported himself from a government job that paid him bare monthly wages to live on. He was nominated for a Nobel Prize.

From among his most popular books is one called *Nosso Lar (Our Home)*. He wrote it in 1943, and it has sold over two million copies and become so famous that a movie called *Astral City* was made of it. The movie is available from Amazon and is also listed on the movies to watch at the end of this book. It is a fascinating movie about the workings of a spirit colony, the first such movie I have had an opportunity to watch. The message of how to live our lives with love, compassion, and help toward one and all, while on earth, comes through very loud and clear. The fact that the drama of our lives and its unfolding is karmically linked by our own daily actions in this and previous lives and their resultant entanglements is beautifully portrayed. It also shares that we are always being watched, loved, and helped by our spirit guides.

It would be impossible for an illiterate man to come up with concepts and explanations that Chico covers in his books unless he had external help. The clarity and depth of his understanding as reflected in his books is very impressive, in my humble opinion, as is the consistency of the basic message of love and compassion for us humans. The play of our actions (karma) and their results, our cause and effect, in our lives here and in the hereafter is a central theme in his works as communicated to him from the spirit world.

We in the United States had our version of Chico Xavier: an uneducated farm boy by the name of Hudson Tuttle (1836–1910) living in Ohio who, through automatic writing, wrote all his extraordinary books—well over twenty. One by the name of *Origin and Antiquity of Physical Man* was quoted several times by none other than Charles Darwin in his own book *The Descent of Man*. Darwin, who had no sympathy with psychic matters, was completely unaware of Hudson's capabilities, as was the rest of the world for a while. This episode and so many other similar and different topics are covered so eloquently in a really-well researched book by Gina Cerminara, *Insights for the Age of Aquarius*, written over forty years ago.

CHAPTER 22

The Phenomenon of Ze Arigo, Psychic Surgeon with a Rusty Knife

ON JANUARY 11, 1971, Arigo died at the young age of forty-nine in a violent head-on collision that he saw coming. Before this event was to unfold, for many months he told his family and friends that he often saw a black crucifix, implying that his mission and work on earth was coming to an end. It was a sign from the spirit world, he would say, from where he had a medical doctor in spirit by the name of Dr. Adolf Fritz overshadow him for many years so Arigo could operate on and help heal people for free. It is estimated that Arigo, in his short time, helped over two million Brazilian poor and often not-so-poor people heal and get well, some from almost near-death illnesses. Unlike John of God who gets entranced and overshadowed by up to thirty-five different entities from the spirit world, including medical doctors, Arigo only had this one rough and gruff German doctor who called himself Dr. Fritz, who had died in World War I.

I should mention here that the main reason, in my mind, that all spirit entities, be those of JOG, or Dr. Fritz, who come to help humanity via their selfless actions and efforts do so they can keep raising their vibrations in whatever sphere or spirit dimension they currently reside to keep ascending ever higher and closer to the light, love, or intelligence we call God. This is our journey, too. We are all part of that same journey.

As a poor young child working on the farms, Arigo started getting blinding headaches and often could hear voices talking to him, sometimes in a foreign language. He tried to block these events whenever they would start but couldn't stop them. He would run inside the house and start crying most times. Later Dr. Fritz was to tell Arigo that he had to work on him for a very long time to finally be able to start overshadowing him successfully. Dr. Fritz, while discarnate, did not feel that his sudden death during the war had finished his mission on earth to help people. So after looking for a while, he found a vessel clean enough mentally and emotionally, in Arigo, to incorporate in him and continue with his work of helping people on earth. Arigo was practically uneducated, and that's why Dr. Fritz said he chose him. It would eventually be very easy for Dr. Fritz to bypass his simple and uncomplicated conscious thinking mind to overshadow him.

Each early morning Arigo would walk past hundreds of sick and often dying patients already lined up waiting outside the door of the Spiritist center where he used to operate, often showing up in muddy shoes. He would simply open the door and people would start walking in quietly. He would then go behind a curtain, close his eyes, and pray to Jesus, and Dr. Fritz would immediately overshadow him. He would then reappear with a completely different demeanor and voice and style of behaving and operating. Apparently, Dr. Fritz when alive was very rough on how he used to operate on his patients, and Arigo would, being overshadowed, simply mimic that. With glazed eyes and newfound speed, he would reach out for any of the available sharp kitchen knives, often rusty ones; a pair of scissors; or any other sharp tool in his rusty tin container sitting on his old desk and start his daily work.

Arigo (like John of God) had grown up in a Catholic family and town and Catholic surroundings. He used to attend church religiously with his family. Initially, in his early work, he was to get imprisoned a couple of times just like John of God did until the authorities and the local church realized and understood the selfless work each of these special and rare full-trance mediums was performing, helping humanity at the behest of the spirits. Neither chose this work. Rather they were handpicked and chosen, and in the case of Arigo, much against his will.

Arigo simply had a photo of Jesus Christ hanging on his wall in the room within the local Spiritist center where he used to perform his work. He became so famous in a very short amount of time that many reputed and skeptic doctors from within Brazil and even outside watched his work from very close proximity. He was also filmed many times. A famous United States psi researcher and medical professional by the name of Henry K. Puharich, MD, had visited him on several occasions with his investigative team. Nobody ever got sick because of Arigo using sharp kitchen knives, including rusty ones, to perform his operations, each of which lasted an average of two minutes or less. Before his day at the office would start, he would have seen over two hundred patients, operated on many of them, written elaborate prescriptions for medications long not used in the medical community but only locally available because Arigo, or Dr. Fritz, was still prescribing them.

He was known to stick a rusty knife right under a patient's eyelid, often pop the eye out a bit, and move the knife around, if needed, to try and find what he was looking for. Often he would leave the knife hanging in the patient's eye as he would turn his head to look at the next waiting patient. Once done with the first patient, he would then wipe the knife clean on the patient's shirt and turn around and start the same procedure on the next waiting patient, using the same rusty knife. No patient ever complained of pain, much less an infection, in all the cases he ever did. This is a documented fact. There are so many others. If you are interested in researching and reading more about Ze Arigo, the best book I have come across is one out of print by John G. Fuller, *Arigo: Surgeon of the*

Rusty Knife, with an afterword by Henry K. Puharich, MD. It was written over forty years ago, in 1974.

None of this, of course, can be explained by our science of today, at least not yet. Our science based on Newtonian physics is only about three hundred years old, while humanity has been walking this earth, accruing and accumulating its collective experiences, for many thousands of years longer. All we have to do is keep an open mind to all that we still don't know and need to discover but acknowledge in full humbleness that the glass often in such cases could be half full. Most of us surely look at life with hope even when we are down and out (i.e., we tend to look at life and its prospective future as a glass half full). Why not try to do the same in such very unique cases one encounters? Simply stay open to receive, process, and experience the experience. Isn't that what our life really is?

I remember being so happy in my life and living high and ecstatic most of the time during this period of discovery. I shared the story of Arigo with many people I was in touch with during that time.

C H A P T E R   2 3

Second John of God Visit
(July 27–August 24, 2014)

MY FIRST TRIP to John of God was so intense and useful that I decided to go again to further deepen my work of self-purification. This time, instead of two weeks, I decided to go for four. My nature, since childhood, is that if I truly like something, I try to go as deep as I can to fully be able to put my arms around the phenomenon, whatever it may be—sales and marketing during my early Silicon Valley years, Wall Street after that, or spirituality now. I will keep doing what I like doing till I am done doing it. Till it becomes a part of me. Then I automatically release it to move forward. The goal in the end is to be and stay free of all phenomena. Some of my friends call me Sodeep instead of Sudeep.

I was also well aware that JOG was not getting any younger and knew of no other place on earth that was still such an intense energy vortex. I now knew the setup and functioning at the Casa pretty well and didn't feel the need to participate in one of Heather's tours. I didn't have any physical ailment and so didn't really need to communicate much with the incorporated JOG anyway. If needed, one of the local Casa translators could suffice if I had any basic questions. My real interest this time was to sit in the different current rooms to experience the intensity of each and just keep cleaning myself within for a month. That was the goal.

I decided to stay at the small Pousada Austria and have my three meals per day at the Pousada Caminho Encantado, about a five-minute walk from the Casa. My room was overlooking the valley in front of me and the highway further down. I was paying about fifty dollars per day, and it included three meals, weekly room cleaning, and laundry service, and this sounded like a good deal to me. I would tip the lady who used to come clean my room and do my hand laundry every week really well. She didn't know any English, but she would bow and shake her head, say something in Portuguese I couldn't understand, laugh, and walk away happy. The day I was leaving, after my month-long stay, I gave her some extra money. I remember her eyes lit up, and she started jumping up and down. Franz, the Pousada owner, who was standing close-by and knew both of our languages, started laughing, telling me she would go shopping that day with the money. I gave her a big hug.

Hugging comes so easy in Abadiania. The more our insides are clean and pure, the more we see the essence of human beings as one and the same, just like each of us, and we truly come to understand in our heart that hugging is our innate nature signifying true oneness among humanity. I also remember, almost daily when JOG was sitting, after coming out of my meditations, I would give money to and hug some of the female beggars sitting outside the gate selling embodied handkerchiefs, hats, and other little trinkets. The more I gave of myself, the happier I felt. I was truly ecstatic and dancing with life.

I had also brought along a couple of really good books to read, a yoga mat, and my protein shake to have with my breakfast. I was good to go.

This time around the Casa felt like coming back home, very familiar. My off days were spent taking small tours to adjoining towns to see the area, jogging, reading, and doing my daily yoga. It really felt like I was permanently living in Abadiania. Sometimes I would go for really long runs behind the Casa, in the hills. I would keep going for miles without seeing anyone. It felt beautiful and very freeing. I had my laptop, my stocks were doing really well, and life was good. I also met some really interesting and fun people, mostly from Austria and Germany since this *pousada* was owned by Franz, an Austrian.

On days when JOG was sitting, I would line up early in the morning in the meditation line to find my favorite spot to sit as close as I could to JOG. It seemed like that was what everyone else was trying to do, thinking, like me, that closer is somehow better.

Before coming on this trip, I went on Amazon and reviewed every book written on or about JOG and made sure I read it, thinking that I did not want to miss any nugget of information about JOG or the early workings of the Casa if available. One book I read was one of his earliest books, *The Miracle Man,* by Robert Pellegrino-Estrich. In it I remember reading many scientific studies done by local Brazilian doctors or organizations. Many such studies never got translated into English, but the author did his best to translate the gist of some of them, and they all said the same thing—JOG is a real phenomenon, not a fraud, though not explainable by science yet. There was one cool study done by an American organization on aura measurements of JOG while incorporated versus when he was not.

While unincorporated, JOG's aura reached out over twelve times the aura of a normal healthy human being (0.45 meters). When incorporated, his aura reached out to over nineteen times that of a normal healthy human being (when incorporated by the spirit of Dr. Oswald Cruz).

While I was there this time, I barely felt the need to get any more crystal bed sessions. I felt pretty aligned, charged, and clean inside.

While I was in Brazil on this trip, my convertible dark-blue Porsche 911 ended up being in an accident. The right side of the car was damaged as it apparently slid across a guardrail. No one was hurt, but I ended up losing my car of fourteen years that I had bought brand new when

You Are Love

I was a senior analyst at Chase H&Q in San Francisco. My body-shop guy in San Rafael and I tried to save the car, but the expense of repairs would have been higher than the residual value to the car, so the insurance company refused and sent me a check for the residual. The body-shop guy tried to coax me into spending money from my own pocket to save the car. When I told him it was, in the end, "all metal and glass" anyway, he looked startled and reminded me it was a Porsche. I smiled and added, "Still metal and glass, brother." He didn't look amused. I had the car for fourteen years, but the universe was telling me it was time to let it go, and I did.

I have continued to let go of a lot of stuff—mental, physical, and emotional—along my now almost ten-year journey of self-transformation. Till we let go, we can't feel lighter and freer within. In my experience, it also doesn't matter the duration of our spiritual or religious practice. The sense of freedom within will not show up till we actually start letting go, physically, mentally and emotionally of all our stuff within.

Since this is important, I will say it in another manner. From my own direct experience, I know that till I started letting go, my spiritual journey hadn't even begun in earnest. Then I was still worshipping with my lips and not my heart, as Salim the Sufi I had met in Delhi by the Dargah, earlier in the book, had reminded me. And as I reflect back on my accelerated conscious evolution of the last almost ten years, I can say with confidence that this journey of ours from our heads to our hearts is the only one that matters in the end. Can we live what we know to be true in our heads in our daily living and interaction? That is the litmus test of our progress and evolution in the end.

Before leaving, I was very happy to see a photo of Jose Valdavino at the Casa shop, which I could not find on my first visit. Valdavino was the third remaining entity who had come through for me during my first visit to JOG. I bought his photo along with a photo of Mary and Santa Rita, the patron saint of the Casa. When Joao was a poor young adult, it was Santa Rita who had incorporated for him and told him to go to a certain Spiritist center where people were waiting for him so they could be healed, and that first incorporation and healing by him started his work and mission. If I recall, King Solomon was the one who overshadowed him that first time. I also bought a couple more rosaries.

By the time I was done with the second trip, I had consumed a lot of herbs that are prescribed to pretty much everyone who visits the Casa and sees JOG. I had consumed from my two trips, a total of six big bottles of capsules and two small ones. The big bottle had 175 capsules, and the small one 35. I am sure at some level they also helped me purify from within.

After getting back from the trip, I heard from some people that their ailment got cured when they visited JOG, but it came back some time after their return back to their daily routine. To experience the healing energy at JOG is like getting an intense spiritual shower. It dissolves our mental and emotional blocks within as much as we let go and allow while there. If we don't change our habits, then soon, because of them, our mental and emotional blocks start accumulating within us again. We have total control over this process. A profound shift in our behavior and thinking needs to take place. As we become kinder, gentler, more loving, and forgiving toward ourselves and others, we allow more of this healing energy always around us—much more intense at JOG of course—to keep cleaning, purifying, and healing us on a daily basis wherever we live. This is what I tell my clients as well, both of life coaching and those who come for energy healing.

As I said earlier, I found on returning from my first JOG trip, even during my short fifteen-to-twenty-minute meditations at home or in front of my altar, I started feeling this same energy that I first became aware of sitting in the Casa meditation rooms, fully and strongly coursing through me. I now rarely sit in formal meditation because my whole daily living is a meditation. During the day, this energy often takes over me and makes me close my eyes, and I sit quietly and let it keep purifying me. It is the most peaceful and calming feeling. This energy is available to each one of us all the time. I don't have to go anywhere to experience it. All I need to do is clean myself of my mental and emotional defilements enough so as to allow this healing energy to course through me more fully.

Sudeep Balain

I distinctly remember on my way back from my second JOG trip, while waiting in the Miami terminal for my flight to SFO, I fell into a deep trance, sitting right there on my seat, for over half an hour. That same very intense intoxication took over me. I felt drunk with love and in the intense grip of this energy or force field again. I couldn't move. One almost becomes like a statue. This energy is available everywhere to us once we are open to it. The whole experience was extremely strong and, I still distinctly remember, had the same tingling effects and the physical coursing of energy sensations in my whole body, especially my forehead, the top of my head, my arms, my hands, and my palms. I can actually feel this energy circling in my palm chakras. I know it is this same energy flowing through me (and each one of us) that I am able to heal with.

I have read about the Kundalini awakening episodes of some people, especially of Gopi Krishna, in his autobiography. The only difference in my such experiences, if I can call them Kundalini awakening or manifestation experiences, is that I have never felt any associated pain anywhere in my body so prevalent and elaborately mentioned by others during their experiences. I only feel an abundance of bliss, wholeness, connectedness, and sheer unconditional love for all in a much more heightened and intense way.

CHAPTER 24

Communications from
the Spirit World

By RESEARCHING THE field of near-death experiences (NDEs) quite thoroughly, the phenomenon mentioned earlier in the book, I knew there was a part of us that survives death—call it soul, energetic, or etheric body that disengages from our physical at death while retaining the whole human personality. It is via this much-lighter, fluffy body that the NDErs then experience the tunnel effect, encountering warm and loving beings of light and often deceased family members. Depending on how long the NDEr is down, he or she gets a brief tour of what definitely sounds like another hard-to-describe, enchanting, and very loving dimension. On reading experiences of Eben Alexander, Anita Moorjani, and so many others, one is left with no doubt. Often then, the NDEr decides of his or her own volition to return back since his or her work or mission in the current life is not yet complete. Always on returning to the physical body in our dimension, the just relived and hard-to-explain, enchanting experience is sorely missed and fondly remembered, often shared via some great books. Sometimes I have read accounts of such patients getting so upset over being brought back into their physical bodies that they start yelling at their doctors about why they helped facilitate it. Clearly these spirit-world experiences for such patients seem to simply be out of this world.

I wanted to take my understanding and learning beyond this first phase. What happens next? Is there surely life after death, and if so what does it feel like? What will I be doing up there in another dimension after my death? Does my state of mind at death determine which higher dimensions in the spirit I would get to live and experience? Such questions, propelled by my insatiable curiosity, led me to open a new and amazing door where I studied and researched high-caliber mediums and often the spirit guides who came through them to identify consistency in their message.

Below is a summary of their essential message, in my words, essentially our way forward. My observations are in parentheses. To construct the dialogue that follows, I have referred to all the books on mediums, healers, regression therapists, and spirit communications mentioned in the list at the end of the book in the appendix.

One word of caution to the reader—in your own investigations and research into this phenomenon, I would highly recommend that you read the actual biographies and often autobiographies of such mediums and not simply rely on reading whatever shows up when you Google their names. Often the information I encountered on the Internet was wrong and utterly false.

- ° The spirit controls (of mediums) often repeat the great importance of cause and effect in our lives: that it is a universal law. We are always in complete control of our destinies, and only through our own actions in past and current lives do we get to enlarge our self-created web of karmic ups and downs and their resultant unfolding that we get to untangle in each life. Nothing in life is an accident.

- ° As our spiritual understanding continues to grow, we increase the control we give to our spirit (soul) within to control our lives. This greater authority we give to our spirit within gets to increase our auric field around us, which thereby gets to increase the communication ability of our conscious mind so it gets to interact that much farther out with other atmospheric thought waves beyond its earlier range. (This clearly hints to the presence of knowledge availability for our conscious minds all around us.)

- ° Our physical apparatus and thinking brain is driven by our spirit within and its constant interface without (almost implying that our brain is simply an organ, a receiving and processing instrument governed principally from its outside interface).

- ° When we close our eyes in death, we will be the same person when we wake up in spirit on the other side. (This I have read to be true via many other sources. That we get to retain our personality as is at the moment of death. Just because we have died, this doesn't change who we are. Yes, our experiences get to be much more heightened in the other dimensions, but who we are stays the same, implying that again we are in full control of our journey here and in the hereafter. This surely implies that it is critical to die well, and to do that, it is critical to live well.)

- ° Our earthly work of transcending our desires and dissolving our negative emotions of hatred, anger, envy, and other such defilements of our mind should take front seat in our daily efforts of living. (This is a reminder again and again to be the primary purpose of why we are here.)

- ° All spirit controls say that they can only talk about what they have experienced to be true for each of them being at the spirit level that they currently are. They say that there are clearly many more levels above them where spirits of much-higher order reside based on their higher wisdom and understanding attained through their own self-work. And that such much-higher dimensions of vibrations are not accessible to these spirit controls who came through to give the messages (implying that we are vibrationally contained to the spirit dimension in the spirit world based on our level of spiritual attainment and freedom gained).

- ° They also mention that those who believe while on earth that death is a long sleep and they will only wake up when the "trumpet sounds" will continue to sleep for a very long time till they are themselves ready to do the work of their self-awakening and enlightenment.

- ° There is no judging or punishment. We do whatever we do in the spirit world of our own accord to better ourselves whenever we feel we are ready for change. Everybody has to pass through and experience the same stages of learning in their eternal growth, here and in the hereafter.

- ° Heaven is described as this indescribable unity with a divine whole that is beyond description. They tell us that whatever is our most perfect experience on earth, to multiply it by millions of times to give us a sense of what this ecstasy and joy would feel like. This experience naturally depends on our own spiritual progression and work and, thus, rung on that spiral ascending ladder. Spirit controls add that the more we can learn to forgive the faster we make it up this ladder. (It's almost like forgiveness extends our receptive reach.)

◦ The best way to stay healthy and disease free is to stay open-minded. An open mind encounters fewer conflicts along the way and thus less accumulation of stress, which is the real cause of our energy blocks, which eventually manifest as physical disease.

◦ Earth is simply a school, and we get to come here to learn to perfect ourselves time and again on our eventual journey of enlightenment.

◦ Each of us on earth is being guided by our spirit guides.

◦ Religious bigotry, bias, and clinging to physical life are part of our ignorance that continues to limit us here and in the hereafter.

◦ We decide before coming in each life our purpose (prarabdha karma to untangle), drama (our possible opportunities to untangle), and actors (people with whom we have tangled karma to untangle) with the help of our spirit guides. Our free will is in how we act and react to our daily unfolding life events. (This I have also read about through the regression work done by therapists and what their clients bring through in hypnosis.)

◦ Our suffering comes only when we don't accept the inevitable changes in our daily lives that are offered as opportunities to help purify us.

◦ Love is nonpossessive and unconditional.

    °   Our unsatiated human desires at death and our fear of death act to slow down our growth on the other side.

    °   The greatest crime we can commit as human beings is to deliberately and intentionally set out to hurt and victimize others, especially people who are helpless and cannot defend themselves. (The key word here is intention—what is our intention in our every action?)

Everything fits perfectly. The message is essentially the same and often given in different ways, and it is always about love, peace, mutual respect, harmony, equality, and sharing being the common denominators of all humanity. At a deeper level, there is no black or white or brown—we are all human beings first, here to experience and fulfill our unique mission of learning, growth, and contribution to each other and to humanity.

As I also researched all the true religions that human beings have embraced since the start of time, I learned that the prophets who started them had this same basic message for all of us: a message of love, sharing, equality, personal effort, and an innate knowing that we are all made in the image of God as love and light.

In *The Gospel According to Thomas*, "Jesus said: 'If people ask you, Where have you come from? Tell them, 'We have come from the Light, from the place where the Light is produced.'"[1]

All these mediums (via their spirit guides), regression therapists, NDErs, and the great sages and yogis of all times and religions, could not all be colluding together to give us this same basic message over our last thirty-five-hundred-year human history that I researched. That didn't make any sense to my open, rational, and educated mind. On top of that, in our own individual self-realizations, we get to experience this same unconditional love and equality toward all humanity within us. This basic message of love and sharing simply had to be true.

The only other thing I will add here is that in all my readings and research of spirit communications so far, no one in that world seems to have seen what we call God. They describe what we call God as a universal essence or higher beings of light but do not assign anthropomorphic qualities to it. They speak of the glory of this essence and its infinite love. But the God of the spirit world seems to be impersonal (i.e., available to one and all who strive to get closer to it by their own efforts of self-purification). It seems to be one whole, undifferentiated and indivisible, though called by many names.

Before I leave this chapter, I will recommend you, dear reader, read a book, especially if you are in the medical profession, that really opened my eyes to all of what is possible from the spirit world. The book *Healing Hands* is a true story of an English doctor. It is an out-of-print book but can be bought on Amazon. The story is similar to that of Ze Arigo of Brazil that I discussed earlier in the book, but this phenomenon occurred in our Western world this time.

In this amazing book written by J. Bernard Hutton in 1978, you will meet Dr. Lang, the main spirit who was a known and established doctor in the United Kingdom while alive. People living who knew him attested to that. He and his friends on the other side, in the spirit world, after a long search, find a local fireman, George Chapman, as the ideal human to overshadow for the continuation of their work on earth. Dr. Lang always worked on the patient's spiritual bodies, a couple of inches above the physical, and said that from there the effects of his operations would permeate into the physical body of the patient. And, of course, they did, each time.

George, while overshadowed, would take on the exact demeanor and mannerisms of Dr. Lang, even the way Dr. Lang used to walk when alive. With eyes completely shut during the whole process, George (as Dr. Lang) would perform the invisible operations on the energetic body of his patients, just a couple of inches above the physical. To the patient lying down and looking up, all he or she would see were George's hands opening and closing as if grabbing instruments and giving them back during an actual hospital operation, all the while his eyes being completely shut. Some of his patients heard his invisible metal instruments as he went along merrily. It's a very well-documented true story. For those who say there is nothing in us except our physical body, I ask you to please keep an open mind and read this book.

One last thing I will mention before we leave this chapter. Apparently, our loved ones in spirit are able to see our futures that seem to have played out in some dimension, clearly not ours. They can predict our future 100 percent correctly, every time. Often such predictions come through a medium who then relays it to the client. I have read about this in innumerable books, written by different authors and during different time periods. Maybe this is why astrology, which is considered a science in India, often works so well. This also reminds me of Dr. Lang, discussed above, who used to perform his spirit operations always on the energetic body of his patients, couple of inches above the physical, and the operations and their resultant healing would then permeate and get impressed onto the patient's physical body. Maybe something similar might also be at work in relation to our phenomenal world and our active role in it. Our future being ahead of our present, and having already manifested in another dimension, continues to get impressed onto our physical dimension and reality every moment, moment to moment.

CHAPTER 25

Becoming a Reiki Master Teacher and Healer, 2014

DURING THE START of June 2014, after much looking, I found the Reiki teacher I was to get my mastership from, literally in my backyard in Tiburon. The whole three attunements and the mastership took till the first week of March 2015 to finish. It was a great experience for me, and Reiki healing came naturally to me. I think part of the reason for this was that by time I started, I had purified myself enough within that the Reiki or universal energy just flowed uninterrupted through me. This seems to be true in general as well. The cleaner we are within, the stronger this current flows through us so we can help heal others. By cleaner I mean unconflicted within, in harmony with ourselves, and generally peaceful.

Caroline Thibeaux of Kinetic Waves also was an amazing Reiki teacher for me. Reiki healing just came naturally to her as a gift. To test this before I signed up for Reiki 1 with her, I decided to get a Reiki healing session from her. That one-hour session with her working on me was very effective. I felt really intense energy flowing through me via her hands. Having been to John of God twice by now, completing two Vipassana courses and all the meditations I had done so far, I knew what intense meant. As we finished the session, I asked her if she would train me. Such training in the Reiki lineage is never a given. The teacher also has to make sure the student is ready, able, and serious. Luckily, I was all three.

Reiki is a Japanese art of healing rediscovered by Dr. Mikao Usui in Japan. It is a natural noninvasive form of activating and reenergizing a client's own bodily life-force energy such that it results in an experience of holistic wellness for the client. Reiki, in my experience, works really well for all kinds of aches and pains throughout the body. As this channeled energy removes energy blocks from within my client's body, he or she feels more centered, rested, calm, and often energized. Depending on the intensity of pain or healing required, it can take a couple of days and multiple sessions to alleviate the pain. Often people I have done Reiki on see images in their mind's eye, like the example of Susan I gave earlier in the book, who saw during her Reiki session the image of Yukteswar and a lion. The more open we are, the more we allow this energy to come through us to heal. The nature of this energy is to heal. I often use my own hands on myself to heal very successfully.

During Reiki 1, it was one other student and me with our teacher Caroline. I liked that it was a small group. I always tend to learn better in smaller groups. We did a lot of practice sessions on each other and on Caroline throughout the day. We got started at nine in the morning and didn't finish till five that afternoon. We were having so much fun; the whole day flew by. During one of the practice sessions, it was my turn to lay hands gently on Kathy, the other student, to sense her bodily energy and see if I could pick up anything. She was lying flat, faceup on the massage table. As I started from her head and worked down her body, I sensed she was drawing in a lot of energy. I could easily tell this as I felt palpable sensations of energy actually leaving my hands through my fingers and through the circular movements of energy in my palm chakras.

It is a very physical and real feeling for me. My arms, hands, and palm chakras are alive and tingling as this energy flows through me. I also feel this same tingling on my forehead, crown chakra, and probably all over my body if I take notice of it. Usually, my focus is on my arms, hands, and palms.

We did many cool experiments during the day to sense energy around each other. One was where Caroline wrote a feeling on a Post-it note and shared it with Kathy for her to start experiencing within herself. Of course I was not shown what that word was each time. My task was to move my hands around her head, neck, and shoulder areas without touching her to see if I could correctly pick up what she was feeling. This time we were sitting on chairs facing each other. As soon as Caroline showed the first word to Kathy, I closed my eyes and got a thought that the word was *anger*. I then got up and slowly moved my cupped hands around her. I didn't have to; I knew the feeling already. As I said aloud, "Anger," I was very surprised that I gotten it right so easily. I got the next word right away as well. It was *love*. Over time, as I practiced more, I realized how much information is stored in our auras and in our various energetic bodies (fields) in and around our physical bodies.

I was on to something. I was discovering as I went along that day that this was my natural talent. Caroline was very excited for me as well and agreed that healing people is where I was headed as a profession. It came so naturally to me. I remember her saying, "You'll be a great healer and help a lot of people."

We did more hands-on exercises for Reiki 2, this time with symbols that we could evoke to help us heal. It got a bit more tedious having to learn the exact way to draw the symbols and their correct way of usage. With Reiki mastership we got more power symbols to use. It definitely got much harder, but I kept going. There were three students for Reiki 2 and two for mastership.

As I reflect back on my past almost ten-year journey of self-transformation, it is even amazing to me to see how much distance I have covered during this time. Here I was working in marketing in Silicon Valley; traveling to Japan, Singapore, and Korea; peddling nonvolatile semiconductor chips; helping run an over-$200-million product line;

and then pushing and pulling on Wall Street for so many years, working first on the sell side and then the buy side at mutual funds and hedge funds and then starting my own hedge fund, and now here I was sensing energy on my student partner, seriously enjoying learning Reiki. I had never felt more fulfilled and happier in my life. I felt completely connected with myself and thus everyone around me.

As I went deeper in my Reiki healing work, I truly understood the role stress plays in our daily lives to perpetuate disease if that stress is allowed to accumulate. There is so much medical science now supporting this basic thesis. It is of utmost importance in my opinion and experience that our stress needs to be dissolved on an ongoing basis, not just through physical exercises, which are a must, but also through other healing modalities like physical massages and energy healing, including Reiki. The holistic approach to healing the whole human mechanism is paramount—mind, body, and soul together.

I want to mention to you, dear reader, couple of book I highly recommend if you want to increase your overall understanding of the spirit world, natural wellness and healing abilities. The first one is *Mind to Mind* by Betty Shine, whose name I have mentioned earlier as well. I have recommended this book to many friends who are in the healing-and-wellness profession. This book is an amazing read on many fronts. I personally use some of the techniques and exercises she mentions in the book in my own healing work. I also remember talking about her to my massage therapist Audrey at Massage Envy, who then really wanted to read the book but didn't have access to Amazon. Knowing it is an out-of-print book, I just ordered it for her and took it with me on my next session.

The second book is an autobiography of Ena Twigg, another very accomplished British medium. The book, *Ena Twigg:Medium*, is a fascinating read on many levels. In it among other things, you will encounter an interesting live thought-communication that Ena had with our President Kennedy, of course since his death. She also mentions the time when she saw the actual materialized face of Martin Luther King, while his dear wife was giving a speech in his honor that Ena was watching on TV. She felt a presence, turned around and was looking at his face and heard him speak, supporting his wife. This book written in 1972, is also out of print but is available via Amazon.

Because this chapter is on healing, I want to bring it to a close with a recommendation of Ambrose and Olga Worrall, an American couple who were clairvoyant healers and who, while living in Baltimore, tirelessly helped heal thousands of people for over fifty years without charging a fee for their work. Ambrose passed away in 1972 and Olga in 1985. Their true story can be found in two of their insightful books: *The Gift of Healing* and *Olga Worrall: Mystic with the Healing Hands*.

From the perspective of quantum nonlocal communication and the effectiveness of prayer, I will mention briefly a really interesting scientific experiment that I came across in *Olga Worrall: Mystic with the Healing Hands.*

Among many experiments performed during the lifetime work of Ambrose and Olga Worrall, there was one performed in 1967 by a Dr. Robert Miller (particulars below) to see if the growth of a new blade of rye grass could be accelerated simply by the Worralls focusing their thoughts on it. Before the experiment was to be conducted, growth of the blade of rye grass had stabilized at 6.25 mils per hour (0.00625 inches per hour). All the laboratory conditions of temperature, lighting, humidity, and so forth were strictly maintained and supervised. Both the Worralls, during their nightly 9:00 p.m. silent prayer time (of just five minutes), visualized the plant growing strongly.

The next morning, they made observations from the trace on the strip-chart recorder. It was found that before the scheduled prayer time, the trace was a straight line with the slope showing a growth rate of 6.25 mils per hour. At 9:00 p.m. sharp the night before, the trace began to move upward, and by 8:00 a.m. the following morning, the growth rate was 52.5 mils per hour, an increase of 740 percent. The experiment was continued for another two days, during which the growth rate slowed down but never returned to its original rate. The Worralls were sitting six hundred miles away from the blade of grass.

If a blade of grass can be influenced at such a distance by our thoughts, imagine what our thoughts are doing to the cells in our bodies so much closer by. We indeed have control over the well-being of our physical apparatus through our everyday thought processes.

The abovementioned scientific experiment is also mentioned in greater detail along with many others by Dr. Robert Miller in his small book *Miracles in the Making*. Dr. Miller received his BS, MS, and PhD in chemical engineering from The Ohio State University and was professor of chemical engineering at Georgia Institute of Technology for fifteen years.

CHAPTER 26

Mahamudra Teachings

"DRAW WATER, BUT don't get wet,"[1] pretty much sums up the entire teachings of Mahamudra Mahasiddhas (Great Achievers) for me. Live in this world freely (*mukti*) and enjoy it fully (*bhukti*), without getting attached to any of it. The key here is this word: detachment. As soon as there is worldly attachment for the Tantric Siddha, he loses his mukti, his freedom.

This is the essential teaching and end goal of Mahamudra, the highest Tantric Buddhist teachings. Some of the most revered Siddhas, like Tilopa, Naropa, Marpa, and Milarepa, all belong to this lineage. The entire lineage of the so-called founding fathers of Mahamudra saints is a total of eighty-four perfected self-realized beings, all living in India between the eighth and twelfth centuries CE, who perfected, practiced, and passed on their various meditation techniques. These Siddhas came from all walks of life and exemplified the perfection of their spiritual attainments by actually living and enjoying whatever the world had to offer to them without any attachment to it versus sermonizing, renouncing, or indulging in asceticism of the world as practiced by others during those times.

Early on, they also did not believe in external uniformity among them or any formal discipline in their lineage. The principal aim of this Tantra continued to be the freedom from suffering, man's eternal goal.

Tilopa, one of the great masters, is famous to have said that there is nothing wrong with pleasure; it is our attachment to pleasure that brings sorrow.

The challenge posed by Tilopa to us in our modern times is the same as discussed in other places in the book: can we transcend our egos and dance with life every day equanimously? The answer through my own direct experience is a resounding yes!

Can we live in this world and not be of it? Yes.

Can we exist like a lotus flower does in the midst of muddy and dirty waters (the ups and downs of our daily living), ever blooming? Yes.

Can we glide through life effortlessly like an eagle does in the sky? Yes.

Can we be like the broccoli leaf with morning dew drops on it? As the leaf is gently touched, the water rolls right off, leaving no trace. Can we live our daily life exhibiting no scars? Yes.

A stage comes in our flowering when we allow everything to pass through us. We hold nothing in, so there is no room for conflicts to arise from within. And when they do arise, they quickly get absorbed back into the stillness of the lake within. Our egos are the cause of our conflicts. Transcend it now. This is our true work and yardstick of progress in this life.

Detachment and equanimity go together. We keep running into these two words. Everything that I have discussed in this book eventually is about these two words.

CHAPTER 27

Discovering Hasidism

As I STARTED researching and reading more about Judaism, I was drawn immediately to Kabbalah and Hasidism, so I went deeper there. Luckily, a wonderful professor from The Hebrew University of Jerusalem, Gershom Scholem, had already done some major work in investigating and opening the history and mysteries of Kabbalah for a layman like myself. So I started with him. He has written some good scholarly works on Jewish mysticism. Through him I came upon the next chapter in Jewish mysticism, Hasidism, started by the great Baal Shem Tov in eighteenth-century Eastern Europe.

The Baal Shem Tov was one with God and danced in that intoxicated love and bliss in his daily interactions with one and all. It was so amazing and enthralling for me to witness again the same qualities of demeanor and behavior toward one and all that came through the Baal Shem that has also come through other enlightened beings across time and geography once one gets fully intoxicated and connected with God's love within. Be it the Sufis, the Upanishad Vedantists, St. Francis of Assisi, Kabir,

Meera Bai and her love for Krishna, or Ramakrishna, the experience of connecting with God within and without is always the same. It shows up as ecstasy, perpetual bliss, and impersonal right action toward one and all. Suddenly one feels as if in the influence of and being guided by a higher force from within and without. Such was the case of the Baal Shem Tov as well. He loved people, including, of course, his Jewish people.

Baal Shems were faith healers, often mixing their knowledge of Kabbalah in their practices to heal and also drive away bad spirits. In those difficult times in Eastern Europe or much of the world, poor people in villages could not afford a doctor and would often gravitate to such Baal Shems for their healing.

The Baal Shem in his daily dealings with his people stressed the importance of unconditional love for each other and for the Torah of course. He stressed the importance of experiencing God wherever one found oneself, not just when one is in the synagogue. If one has eyes to see, God's *shekina* (presence of God) is everywhere and in everything. He encouraged, inspired, and offered new hope to the Jewish people of his time. He knew he had tasted the love of God within and without, of his Father in heaven, and wanted to share that message with his people as their due right as well. He urged his growing followers to let their prayers not be held down because of their lack of good intentions behind them. Always pray with your heart, not just your lips, so God can hear you, he would often tell them. He used to say that there can be no true service of God without love and joy in it.

To me, in simplistic terms, a Sufi and a Hasid (pious one) are brothers. Both stay ecstatic with the intoxicated love of God within and without and in the process become almost unhinged and detached from the world around them. In fact, this is true of every being of light who dares to travel within fully to explore and taste the sweet waters from that well. That is where God resides in each one of us, as unconditional love waiting patiently to be experienced and expressed.

By the start of the twentieth century, Hasidism was in serious decline. Two philosophers among many, in my mind, tried to bring forth a new vision, to infuse a new strength into Baal Shem Tov's Hasidism. To try and polish it so as to give it new appeal for a newer Jewish community that by then had been through enough persecution, pogroms, and anti-Semitism in most of Europe, but especially in Eastern Europe. The Jews, by then, were without hope and home. These two philosophers were Martin Buber (1878–1965) and Hillel Zeitlin (1871–1942).

Martin Buber focused more on propagating the Baal Shem Tov's Hasidism through his efforts of collecting and assimilating the many old Hasidic tales centered around the Baal Shem and his followers and writing extensively about them.

It was Zeitlin who really took me over with his new vision of Hasidism of the future.

To construct the following dialogue, I have referred to the well-edited and translated book *Hasidic Spirituality for a New Era* by Arthur Green.

Hillel was an extremely bright kid who started studying the Talmud and other legal texts by the time he was eleven. By the time he was thirteen, for about six months, it was as if he was consumed by a divine fire. His ecstasy knew no bounds. He felt he was one with Ein Sof, the formless God of Kabbalah. This state of Hillel, unfortunately, did not last.

As he became an adult and had to work, he got much more disenchanted with the growing fate of his world and Jewish poverty around him. The pettiness and small-mindedness that he encountered of his fellow Jews as well as non-Jews really got to him. There was simply not enough to go around during those times.

Hillel grew up reading Hartmann, Schopenhauer, Baruch Spinoza, Friedrich Nietzsche, the pacifist Tolstoy, Kabbalah, and Hasidism. Over the years, he also studied the Zohar, the principal text of the Kabbalah.

He liked in Schopenhauer the reference to Indian mysticism and the thought of the basic Vedantic principle of God (as Brahman) and man always in unity, not duality as in the Western religions, where God and man appeared separated. Vedanta believes that a part of Brahman is in each of us as a spark of divinity they call Atman.

This initial exposure to Vedanta and later Buddhism was to play a big role, in my mind, in Zeitlin's vision of the future of his Hasidism, which he gradually started to lay out in his writings. All the ongoing pogroms and general devastation that he had been witnessing in the various Jewish communities throughout Eastern Europe really made him a pessimist. In trying to make sense of these outward worldly horrors that no one seemed to be able to control, much less stop, he went more inward to try and deal with this outward show of worldly butchery and aghastness. This is where Buddhism greatly helped him become more functional in his daily life and eventually less pessimistic. By seeing the whole world and its workings as simply an illusion, his mind was trying to make sense and process what his religion then was not showing him a way out of. For a while he became secular.

By the time Zeitlin was in his midforties, he went through another mystical experience like that of his adolescent years. This started to somehow bring him back to his Jewish roots.

By now Zeitlin had started forming his views of what his new version of Hasidism would look like; he called his movement Yavneh. He imagined many such local communities spread out in Eastern Europe and in the Holy Land consisting of youthful Jews committed to living a rarified spiritual life with deep inner meaning and love among its members.

Each such community member would work in a trade, not a business, as he felt any business eventually would lead to lying and cheating, which he saw enough of among his own business people. He is almost reminding me here of the formative years of Gandhi, living in his ashram in South Africa, self-sufficient and self-reliant, where every member was required to do some daily chore and make himself or herself useful. Gandhi, of course, got his inspiration from watching Tolstoy live and write on his farm, walking away from all his wealth and luxury.

The other thing Zeitlin wanted his members of the Yavneh to follow was a simple life of modesty, lacking in luxury. Luxury, he felt, sapped the human mind and misdirected its inherent true potential of high and noble thinking.

There were other directives to purify oneself; not exploit anyone; keep one's family strong, peaceful, and loving; stay humble; meditate; and constantly watch one's speech and outward behavior. Many places in his writings, the need to keep the mind and body pure in thinking and eating is mentioned.

The other person Zeitlin's vision of creating a Yavneh reminds me of is Jiddu Krishnamurti, who is also discussed at length earlier in the book. K never believed big religious organizations were long-term effective in helping people accelerate their process of conscious evolution or self-realization. He also suggested, at different times, the formation of small groups of twenty to twenty-five like-minded individuals who would come together to learn and grow from each other. From such small groups would spread a love, light, and understating to others who come in contact with them, and this way the light spreads gently but surely.

If the reader is interested in investigating Zeitlin more, I would highly recommend the above-mentioned book which is offered by the Classics of Western Spirituality. In it is also a very interesting imaginary conversation between Zeitlin and the Baal Shen Tov, which I thought was very well presented.

Zeitlin was martyred at the Warsaw ghetto in 1942 at the age of seventy-one. He is known to have walked wearing his *tallit* (prayer shawl) and carrying *tefillin* (small black leather boxes containing scrolls of parchment inscribed with verses from the Torah) and a copy of the Zohar in his hand. This is how much he loved the Zohar.

CHAPTER 28

Meditation Circle in Mill Valley

MY FRIEND ANGIE and I started a meditation circle at my house in Mill Valley in 2015. We would meet as a small group of three to five people once a week, usually every Tuesday, if I recall, late mornings once everyone's kids had been dropped off at school. We would sit in my bedroom where my altar is.

I have always liked lighting a menorah, and we'd do it each time we met. One of us would say a prayer of our choosing. Angie would very sweetly often pray in Hebrew, asking for a blessing for our meditation circle. I would play music for about twenty minutes from my iPhone, and we would either sit up straight or lie down during that time and meditate. Often the energy in the room would be very strong for me. The same effects of tingling I had experienced at my first Vipassana course, which then got more intense during my continued self-purification efforts at my first John of God trip, would be with me. As I described earlier, I would also feel this energy coursing all over my body, especially on my forehead, the top of head, my arms, and my hands and palms. Often I would be made to stay absolutely still, as if I had become a stat-ue and couldn't move. I am sure I could have if I really tried, but the effort to try would often get taken away from me. Once we came out of our meditations, we would just sit and talk about whatever came into our thoughts. We would often take our cups of tea to my backyard and sit and talk.

This was our version of Zeitlin's Yavneh. We would share ideas, try to understand the common ground in our everyday ups and downs, and discuss books we were reading. This continued for a few of months, and then ev-eryone went their own ways. I used to call this Yavneh our Prem Salon. *Prem* means unconditional, nonpossessive, or divine love in Hindi, the language spoken by the major-ity in India.

CHAPTER 29

Last Incarnation on Earth

ANGIE MENTIONED IN passing one day the name of Grace, an intuitive psychic reader living close-by in Marin who she had visited and really liked. I, being ever the curious one in such matters, decided to visit her for an experience. My interest in all such psychic encounters, as I have mentioned before, has been less in what is being told but more in how it is being facilitated.

We set up an appointment for the coming week. Grace told me she charged one hundred dollars for a one-hour session, which I was to learn later would often go past the allotted one hour. She was generous with her time.

As soon as she welcomed me into the living room and I sat down, Grace took a crystal from among many sitting on the table and told me it was from John of God's Casa. Then she just took off really fast, telling me what she was picking up from the energy in and around me. Often she wasn't even looking at me, just sensing what was around me. I hurriedly pressed record on my digital recorder I had brought with me. She just kept going.

She was now telling me stuff she saw for my kids that she was apparently sensing in my energy field. My kids were at school, over five miles away. It was really fascinating to see how correct she was in her descriptions of my three kids, their likes, dislikes, and habits. We covered a lot of distance in that over-one-hour session. I let her do most of the talking. I was there to observe and listen and did so.

I distinctly remember, about midway through that session, that she looked squarely at me and just blurted out, "You know, Sudeep—this is your last incarnation on earth."

I didn't know what to do with that. I simply asked, "What do you mean?"

She went on to tell me that after this life I am going to move on to higher dimensions. And she said it in a very matter-of-fact way, as if this was part and parcel of everyone's journey, and I just happened to be toward its end. No big deal.

She also told me that in this life I was often having a hard time dealing with the small–mindedness of people around me. She was definitely right about that. Often in my daily encounters with people, I am made to wonder why, in spite of so much progress in science, medicine, and technology in general, we humans psychologically continue to have such a hard time evolving in our daily behavioral interactions with each other. Where does our free will go when we truly need it in self–reflection to bring out concrete changes and improvements in our lives? We all know what needs to improve within us; we just can't seem to sustain that improvement within us for long. Why is that?

The more I thought about this, the more apparent the answer became. Till we strengthen our foundation within first, anything we try to build on it won't or can't sustain and last. The key is to understand and thus start dissolving our conditioning within first. Till that is done properly and deeply, whatever we try do in our efforts to become nice, kind, or compassionate toward ourselves and others cannot be lasting. I knew this from my own direct experience of the past many years. Soon we are back to our old habits.

I thanked Grace, turned off my recorder, wrote my check, and left. I have since referred a couple of my friends to her, and the ones who have decided to visit her have had productive and often revelatory sessions with her. Not everyone decided to go though.

CHAPTER 30

Patanjali and Sat-Chit-Ananda

IN THIS CHAPTER I want to explore Patanjali's famous *Yoga Sutras* and how they fit into the bigger context of my journey of self-transformation. How, without realizing it, all along on my own journey I was following what Patanjali expected of his disciples that he articulated so well over fifteen hundred years ago.

Patanjali, who is credited to have reformulated the *Yoga Sutras,* which already existed in various forms much before him, lived around second century CE. His *Yoga Sutras* are basically a compilation of four short books, each having a number of aphorisms. The goal of Patanjali through his work was also the same as the four basic forms of yoga efforts discussed earlier—karma, Bhakti, Jnana, and Raja—to achieve *Samadhi, mukti,* self-realization, or union with God within.

To construct the dialogue that follows, I have referred to the book *How to Know God, The Yoga Aphorisms of Patanjali,* translated with a commentary by Swami Prabhavananda and Christopher Isherwood.

Yoga Sutras are comprised of the following four books:

1) Samadhi Pada with fifty-one aphorisms
2) Sadhana Pada with fifty-five aphorisms
3) Vibhuti Pada with fifty-six aphorisms
4) Kaivalya Pada with thirty-four aphorisms

It is interesting that Patanjali starts his very first book with the discussion of Samadhi, his end goal of all spiritual practice. He starts with the highest, the end goal first. In my mind that's the hallmark of a true teacher. Many Upanishads also follow the same rhythm of starting with the highest teaching.

Samadhi in Sanskrit means to place everything together, a gathering of everything in one place. Our mind gets to gather in one place or become one pointed i.e., experience Samadhi, when there are minimal distractions left in it. A state of mind when the seer and seen are one. (The seer is the Atman, the changeless witness within each of us to our daily drama, the God within us, so to say. The seen is our constant drama witnessed in the mind via our five senses). Patanjali says that for such a mind that is disciplined and one pointed, Samadhi is easy to achieve.

He then introduces a new Sanskrit word, Vairagya, which means our state of inner contentment or detachment, not indifference. Patanjali then adds that for a yogi who achieves Samadhi, he automatically, naturally becomes detached because he has become content within. So Samadhi intrinsically creates detachment, which is our natural state of contentment within.

This is a very important distinction in my mind, so let me try to say a few more words on it. According to Patanjali, the primary focus of the yogi is not to become detached in the first place, but to simply become content within. The second state (detachment) comes automatically when the first (contentment) is there. This is the Samadhi Pada.

Let me elaborate and open up the first book a bit more.

The first book deals primarily with laying the Patanjali's groundwork as to why our efforts toward self-realization are so paramount, especially in our modern age of so many distractions, which are additionally adding to our ongoing dissatisfaction. Yoga, as I said earlier, is the union of Sudeep with his higher self within. This higher self can be looked at as God, love, Holy Spirit, or Atman.

So what is coming between Sudeep and his Atman within is Sudeep's ignorance, his ego. Ego as I said earlier is our accumulated psychological thoughts. Unless this ego is understood, this union within is not possible. Sudeep then stays tied to this world and its roller coaster and thus the endless sorrow, and dissatisfaction, leading to lack of equanimity and happiness in his life.

Thus detachment or transcendence from this endless daily roller-coaster ride is essential for our goal of perpetual happiness and freedom, our state of self-realization. Then we can live in this world and fully enjoy and partake of it as the great Mahamudra Siddha's like Tilopa used to do, but because we stay fully detached from our causes of pleasures and happiness, we get to also maintain our much-needed equanimity.

Patanjali talks about the need for meditation and for disciplined hard work to achieve our state of detachment. All this, in many more words and aphorisms, Patanjali then lays out the groundwork or necessity of his *Yoga Sutras* covered in his first book. He also stresses that a direct knowledge of this union within with our higher self is required for our complete freedom and ecstasy, not mere intellectual understanding gained by reading other people's experiences in a book. One has to peel and taste the juicy ripe mango himself or herself to experience its supreme taste and its eternal sweetness.

After whetting our appetites and showing us what is possible in that ultimate state of transcendence and union with God or love within, Patanjali then shows us how to get there, what practices (*Sadhana*) one has to do. This is his second book, *Sadhana Pada*. At the outset here, he says that mere energetic desire alone will not get one there. The yogi has to do Kriya, or perform actions, actually put in the effort to travel toward his or her goal of self-realization. He offers three Kriya practices. These Kriya efforts comprise of our disciplined spiritual austerities that generate Tapas or heat that will burn away our afflictions, our efforts of self-study, and full dedication of the fruits of our such actions to God or a higher Source.

He implies here that for a yogi who is not one pointed and disciplined yet, doing these three Kriyas can get him to Samadhi as well. The goal of these Kriya steps then is to weaken our afflictions, our conditioning. What are our basic afflictions?

Patanjali identifies five obstacles to our enlightenment: our ignorance, egoism, attachment, aversion, and desire to cling to life. Out of all these, our ignorance is our most supreme problem, our biggest impediment. It is our ignorance or lack of realization that *we are already that*—what we are looking for. What we are looking for is already within us, is already a part of us, the Atman, or God as love. All we have to do is remove our ignorance, that it is not, and thus stop seeking it outside of ourselves in things and people. This way with disciplined practice of removing our ignorance by understanding our true nature and removing mental afflictions of our egoism, attachment, aversion and our desire to cling to life, the yogi with time can get to Samadhi as well.

Patanjali having already covered the two ways to get to Samadhi, now suggests that if the yogi is still having a hard time getting to his goal, he should then practice his Astanga, or eight limbs. These eight practices or rules he proposes are his final call for the removal of the impurities of our minds.

These eight practices or limbs of Patanjali's yoga follow:

1) Yama—our five external forms of abstention from evildoing: a) harming others from our thoughts, words, or deeds, b) harming others through our falsehood, c) harming others from our theft, d) harming others from our sexual incontinence or from our lack of moderation or self-control as relating to sex, and e) harming others from our greed

2) Niyama—our five internal observations of purity, contentment, mortification as in subduing one's bodily desires, study, and devotion to God

3) Asanas—our physical yoga postures

4) Pranayama—our breath control via exercises

5) Pratyahara—withdrawal of our minds from sense objects, or making our minds introspective

6) Dharna—concentration

7) Dhyana—meditation

8) Samadhi—absorption in the Atman or love within in ecstatic bliss

Our sustained and disciplined efforts here will show up as our measure of success in what Patanjali then describes in his remaining next two books.

In his third book, the *Vibhuti Pada*, which has another fifty-six aphorisms, he describes the Siddhis, or powers the ardent disciple gets to experience because of all his or her work of self-purification thus far.

The most important power or Siddhi that I as a disciple got to fully realize and experience in my daily living is that of detachment from the phenomenal world of ours. I live, enjoy, and fully partake of all that the world has to offer without becoming attached to it, including its ups and inevitable downs. I become completely equanimous, and whenever that equanimity is momentarily lost, I regain it in no time again. Whenever a stone gets thrown on the lake surface of our minds, in no time the depth of the lake reabsorbs all these new ripples. Such is the immensity and power of this Siddhi.

Patanjali describes the occult powers one gets to experience, which he actually calls obstacles to our experiencing of Samadhi. According to him, once the yogi can really apply his or her deeper efforts of meditation and concentration, he can experience such Siddhis, like walking on water, levitating, mastery over the elements, knowledge of the past and future, and many more such powers. To be honest, some of the Siddhis mentioned in this third book I have never heard of anyone possessing, including all the great self-realized beings that I discuss in this book. To my state of being and life here on earth, they don't even seem relevant, frankly.

The only Siddhis I can attest to beyond my detached state of living as mentioned above, are my really effective healing abilities. My heightened sensing and thought abilities that I first started noticing during my early Reiki learning sessions are also because of my self-purification efforts thus far. From all I have read so far, these are part of our natural human tendencies we get to access from within and without.

Every true saint I know has fully agreed with Patanjali's impatience about making too much of the occult Siddhis discussed in his third book. Too much focus or our indulgence in them to try and activate them simply distracts us from our only eventual goal, which is to attain our self-realization, our mukti, our enlightenment.

There is a well-written book, *Supernormal,* that I read recently from the scientist Dean Radin that discusses the validity of some of these Siddhis from a scientific perspective, if you are interested in investigating this portion more.

Patanjali's last book, the *Kaivalya Pada*, has the remaining thirty-four aphorisms. *Kaivalya* means freedom, or solitude, and this freedom comes about once the illusionary perceived separateness between *purusha* and *prakriti* is understood and, thus, overcome via our *viveka* or discriminative understanding. *Purusha* and *prakriti* can be looked at as analogous to the concept of seer and seen discussed earlier.

Purusha and *prakriti* is again Vedantic terminology where *purusha* is the cosmic unchanging man and can also be by extension looked at as our unchanging and unstainable Atman or higher self within. *Prakriti* is our material, phenomenal, ever-changing world.

For the new self-realized yogi of Patanjali, this illusion-ary separateness collapses, and with it his cycle of birth and death. In other words, Patanjali says that our accumulated Sanchita karma (all the arrows in the quiver) can only be exhausted by our self-realization, only through our own efforts toward our freedom and liberation in the here and now.

According to Vedanta, there are five sheaths or coverings (our conditioning) that hide this higher self (seer) within me from myself, Sudeep. The first is the physical body, the next three constitute the subtle body, and the last is the causal body, closest to the Atman. These are all separate ever-subtler energetic fields. Our Atman, or divine spark, is beyond all of them. As we keep transcending our egos through ever-heightened sense of awareness in our meditations, these sheaths, or *koshas*, become ever finer, thus reflecting more of the nature of the Atman within. No wonder I kept feeling ever more peaceful and blissful the deeper I went within in my meditations and self-purifications efforts over the years.

Once the distance between this seer within me (and each of us) and what is seen, our daily egoic experiences or our identity (Sudeep), is collapsed and transcended, we become one with our higher self. The experience of this union within each of us is always the same, of Sat-Chit-Ananda. The supreme experience of truth within, absolute knowledge, and everlasting bliss. Then the yogi satiated with the peace and bliss derived from this union with Atman shines within and without.

CHAPTER 31

Interconnected

Consciousness and Love

I KNOW THIS really cool guy at the Bay Club who is into ayahuasca, and one day as we were discussing spiritual stuff—our favorite topic—he told me to watch the movie *I Am*, directed by Tom Shadyac, and I did.

The documentary is brilliant on many fronts. It's a must-see.

There is a really cool experiment in which Tom is sitting physically unconnected; by simply projecting his thoughts, he moves the needle of a voltmeter that is connected via electrodes to a petri dish with yogurt, (i.e., live bacteria) in it. Our thoughts are energy. How can the live bacteria in the yogurt pick up Tom's thoughts and register them on the measurement meter if not connected nonlocally with Tom through some kind of invisible medium? Quantum mechanics posits that there is inherent interconnectedness and unity in our universe at a very basic level. Maybe this medium that connects everything to everything else in our universe is consciousness, an invisible fabric or force field that everything rests on and is permeated with. The Vedantic yogis called this consciousness prana or life-force energy, which permeates everything—animate and inanimate.

The movie made me ask some very basic questions: Are we truly separate beings needing to survive and prosper in our world at the expense of others, as Darwin postulated? Maybe our world indeed in not as neatly and orderly separated as Newtonian physics has commanded for the last three hundred-plus years. Perhaps we are all intimately, intrinsically, and immediately connected with each other and everything in the universe at the deepest levels, as the new frontiers of science are also proving.

It has been shown undoubtedly by now, through so many scientific experiments, that plants exhibit and respond to emotions of fear, hatred and love. Even when plants are shielded with a Faraday screen (to intercept all types of electromagnetic radiation), they still register and respond to human emotions, clearly showing an immediate and intrinsic link. A fascinating example is shared in the book of Dr. Robert Miller (who we encountered in chapter 25), *Miracles in The Making*, which shows that plants can read human minds and remember established relationships. In the experiment, two philodendron plants were placed in a room, and six men were asked to enter it. Upon entering, one of the men forcefully uprooted one of the plants and stamped on it. On their leaving, the researcher attached a polygraph to the remaining plant, and the six men were asked to reenter the room one by one. When the "killer" entered the room, the (remaining) plant identified him with a violent and dramatic reaction on the polygraph. The researcher tried to block the communication signals by using a Faraday screen and lead-lined containers to no avail.

In another such experiment, a plant hooked up to a strip-chart recorder had dramatic reactions when it witnessed two friends in the room—who had not seen each other in a while—warmly greet each other, hug, and share a kiss. It was noted on the trace of the recorder that when the two embraced each other, the strip-chart pen went completely off the scale. Expressed love and shared affection released energy that the plant was reacting to.

We also know now that the molecular structure of water changes with expressed thoughts and emotions, such as fear and love. This great work of Dr. Masaru Emoto has been shown so eloquently in the movie, *What the Bleep Do We Know* (also mentioned as a must-see movie in the list at the end of the book). Scientific experiments have also shown that the hydrogen bonding of water changes when the water is prayed over or held by a healer. The human body is composed of approximately 70 percent water. No wonder prayer and meditation work to calm us down and make us more peaceful, connected, and centered.

Could lack of expressed love (and cooperation) in our lives be the answer to all our problems and maladies? I think so, and so do so many others.

You are love. I am love. Could this unconditional love (as a force field) be the fabric that connects everything to everything else?

CHAPTER 32

Karma and Reincarnation

ON WATCHING THE movie, *I AM*, directed by Tom Shadyac, I also learned about Dean Radin (mentioned in chapter 30) and his insightful scientific psychic research and relevant writings in the field of consciousness. Then I went to his website and watched among other things his presentation called "Was Buddha Just a Nice Guy." From that presentation, I learned about the new book of Larry Dossey, *One Mind*. I researched Dossey, liked his work and his various books on healing (my favorite field), and decided to buy his new book.

His concept of one mind "as a collective, unitary domain of intelligence, of which all individual minds are a part,"[1] in my mind is similar to the basic concept of the unity and interconnectedness of Atman with Brahman, that the Upanishadic yogis expounded so thoroughly through their deep meditative experiences over three thousand years ago. Dossey, as he moves further along in his narrative, acknowledges as much in his well-written book.

If Brahman is looked at as undifferentiated consciousness, then each of us having a tiny unit of that same consciousness within us as spirit (Atman) does not sound so far reaching. And that this consciousness connects nonlocally is not far reaching anymore either with the scientific experiments of the last thirty-five-plus years. Also, I know through my own direct experience of self-purification of my conditioning, that the nature of this Atman is unconditional love, a basic attribute we all yearn for, share, and in our own self-realization experience within each of us.

I also liked the fact that Dossey explores with an open mind and gently affirms in the positive the ongoing process of reincarnation, a topic many writers shy away from for fear of offending prospective reader's sensibilities. The reality is that just because I don't believe in reincarnation will not stop this universal process from occurring. In my mind, it is better to understand such universal processes at work than keep trying to ignore them, thinking they will simply go away.

Living in the twenty-first century, we owe it to ourselves and to our higher, more evolved sensibilities to understand as educated and open-minded human beings such basic phenomenon that now have been so well documented for years by Western researchers, not to talk of Hindus who have been believing in it for over three thousand years now. These are the same Hindus who came up with the Vedas, *The Upanishads*, and the *Bhagavad Gita* and innumerable towering spiritually enlightened yogis, some of whom of the last only 150 years are mentioned in this book. These very high quality "experiential" spiritual texts among so many others have unequivocally stood the test of time in their universality of message for all humanity, not just for Hindus.

The basic underlying mechanism at work for these spiritual texts to truly come alive and shine in my mind, especially *The Upanishads* and the *Gita*, and of the teachings of the great yogis I elaborate on in this book, would get much diluted without the acknowledged inherent play of karma and reincarnation in our everyday lives. I think it can only be advantageous and beneficial for us to create space in our individual belief systems for the reality of karma and reincarnation.

In my mind, the reality of karma and reincarnation in our lives and the existence of a spirit world is fairly straightforward. If there is karma (cause and effect), there has to be a way to fulfill it (i.e., our process of reincarnation). If there is reincarnation, there has to be a place to reside after each of our successive physical deaths, so as to continue our process of learning and growth here and in the hereafter.

The ancient Indian scriptures, the Vedas, acknowledge the existence of spiritual dimensions like Brahma Lokas (Abrahamic heaven), where ardent followers of its texts and ritual practices would find themselves upon death. The Vedic followers were keen in living a good, moral life while here on earth and to perform all the required elaborate rituals to make sure they land in heaven after death.

It was later in the Upanishads that followed the Vedas, that there is much clearer commentary on the concept of karma, reincarnation, the necessity of living a wholesome life while on earth, and the definitions of what such a life should entail. So Vedanta clearly concurs with the existence of at least four spiritual dimensions, or *Lokas*, where we get to live depending on our state of mind at death.

It is my firm belief and hope that if more people honestly and with an open mind investigate the phenomenon of cause-effect and reincarnation, more of us will be truly able to make use of our precious remaining time on earth and to utilize it much more productively for our own longer-term benefit. If you don't know what books to read, start where I started with the list I have at the end of the book. That's why I have provided it.

If the reader is interested to understand the "nuts and bolts" of how the process of karma and reincarnation works and effects our daily living, there is no better book in my mind than the one by Gina Cerminara, *Many Mansions: The Edgar Cayce Story on Reincarnation*, first published sixty-five years ago.

Cayce, undoubtedly the greatest American healer of our age, was a deeply religious man of Christian faith who started reading the Bible cover to cover every year from a very young age. To him the Bible indeed had evidence that true life, that of Spirit, is continual. A typical reading of Cayce—and there are thirty thousand such fully documented readings—would go something like this: he would take off his shoes, loosen his tie, fully relax himself, lie down on a couch, and quickly put himself to sleep. One of his trusted helpers then would suggest questions to him about the concerned patient, and Cayce would, after a couple of moments, start giving a full diagnosis of the illness and needed cure. For distant readings, where patients were often thousands of miles away, he additionally only needed to be told the exact name, address, and city of the patient. What followed was the same. At the height of his popularity, he was giving eight readings a day and was often booked out as far as a year and a half in advance. He died in 1945 at the age of sixty-seven. He was a one-of-a-kind, most amazing clairvoyant healer who worked via self-hypnosis.

Cayce initially rejected the idea of karma and reincarnation and only grudgingly embraced it as his readings continued to guide him in that direction. Gina, who herself had a PhD in psychology, spent two long years researching twenty-five hundred of Cayce's psychic readings given over a period of twenty-two years (1923-1945) to formulate her abovementioned book. In her book are highlighted readings after readings of Cayce's patients that intimately relate to the source of their present dilemmas, afflictions, conflicts, and limitations as originating from prior karmic entanglements in past lives. As old as this book is, it is a fascinating read on Cayce and the process of karma and reincarnation. If one truly has an open mind, one is left with no doubt about the inherent and intimate workings of karma and reincarnation in our lives. As Gina mentions in her book, many in the non-Hindu (and non-Buddhist) world of our history have fully accepted the idea of reincarnation: Arthur Schopenhauer thoroughly believed in it, as did Emerson, Walt Whitman, Goethe, Plotinus, Pythagoras, Plato, Virgil, Ovid, Giordano Bruno, Schelling, Leibnitz, Lessing, Fichte, Flammarion, Carlyle, Edison, Luther Burbank, and Henry Ford, to mention a few.

All entangled karma simply needs to be untangled. And that's what each one of us is doing through our daily living, knowingly or unknowingly. I should also add here that karma to me is not punishment but responsibility. Karma is a teaching tool, an evolutionary mechanism, that enables us to keep evolving, to keep opening new doors within us of self-understanding and thus unconditional love.

Because we have free will, we make mistakes in our daily behavior patterns (accrue karma) and thus need reincarnation for our continued development to become whole and complete. It's really this simple.

If we truly understand the underlying mechanism of the ongoing phenomenon of reincarnation, there will be much less discrimination in our lives. There will also be minimal ongoing religious hatred and intolerance that we perpetuate to the next generation. Each of us will deeply understand that we choose to come in each incarnation as peoples of different colors and faith—sometimes black, sometimes white; sometimes Jew, sometimes Muslim; sometimes rich, sometimes poor—simply to experience and complete our learning as each. The goal of each life is to bring us ever closer to becoming whole and complete in God as love. That's all.

Reincarnation is not a Hindu or Buddhist phenomenon; it is a human phenomenon.

In Kabbalah it is called gilgul. If the reader is interested to investigate this phenomenon further in Judaism, I would recommend the book of Gershom Scholem (who we encountered earlier in the book in the chapter on Hasidism), *On the Mystical Shape of the Godhead*. Gershom explains it a bit differently, but it's the same process of reincarnation he is elucidating in Kabbalah. In the book is also a separate chapter devoted to the concept of our astral (etheric) body, which we get to take with us upon death. It is called *tselem* in Kabbalah.

One of the traits of Gershom (and really any author) that I truly admire is that in all his research he shared via his books, his goal was always to follow the truth wherever it led, as he investigated old Jewish texts for the origin and development of Jewish mysticism. His quest was always for historical truth.

We also know now through the works of various reputed Christian scholars that there is a real possibility that Jesus was a student of the Essene community at some point before his brief ministry. Many historical sources also indicate that the Essenes are believed to have taught pacifism, vegetarianism and according to Josephus—the famous Jewish historian—reincarnation. Early Christian documented history also tells us that in sixth century CE, at the Second Council of Constantinople, a group of Christian bishops formally outlawed by vote teachings of reincarnation attributed to Jesus and his ministry.

I will end my commentary on reincarnation with a really succinct quote by Arthur Schopenhauer, the German philosopher mentioned earlier, who has been quoted as an influence to many a great mind of our recent times, like Albert Einstein, Carl Jung, Leo Tolstoy, Erwin Schrodinger, Sigmund Freud, Joseph Campbell, Friedrich Nietzsche, and Thomas Mann, among many others.

Were an Asiatic to ask me for a definition of Europe, I should be forced to answer him: It is that part of the world that is haunted by the incredible delusion that man was created out of nothing, and that his present birth is his first entrance into life.[2]

CHAPTER 33

Prem in My Life, My Mom

MY MOTHER, WHOSE name is Prem, is also the *prem* of my life. *Prem*, if you recall, stands for divine or unconditional love in Hindi. Today she is over eighty-five years old and is in great health and spirits. She has been unconditional love to one and all as her name aptly implies.

My dad and mom were married at a young age when they lived in close-by villages in the state of Haryana in India. When my mom turned eighteen, my dad brought her over to our village. While I was growing up first in Pilani and then in Chandigarh, I don't remember interacting much more with my mom than my dad.

My father was the main center of attraction in our house. He was one of four brothers who lived in Mehlana, all of whom helped till land in those early years, and the whole family lived off the land. Those were simpler times indeed. After finishing his undergraduate and master's in physics, my father decided to head out to America to do his PhD in physics. This was a rather rare feat for an Indian to do in the mid-1950s. He was adamant, very energetic, and really good in his studies, so his two older brothers gathered the necessary funds and sent him to Louisiana State University in Baton Rouge. My father, Kanwal Singh Balain, finished his PhD in barely three years and headed out to Westinghouse, then a large and successful company in Pittsburgh, if I recall. His friends used to call him Ken. Well, Ken worked at Westinghouse for a couple of years and got a few patents in the emerging field of solid state devices, which later were called semiconductor devices.

All this time that my dad was busy working and breaking new ground far away, my mom and my older brother, Anand, and sister, Rita, were living at our ancestral house in Mehlana with my two uncles and their families. I was born after my father returned from the United States in 1962.

I had an amicable and happy, but not exceptionally close, relationship with my mom growing up. I was much tighter with my dad. My mother, in hindsight, has always been the same, with equanimous love for one and all, always happy to be in the background with nothing to prove.

My mother's real depth of wisdom and spiritual attainment I only came to fully understand and appreciate after my dad passed away in March 2008, and really when I started coming up for sustained air, around the middle of 2008, from my depth of personal pain and suffering. As I started experiencing more sustained bouts of happiness and overall wellness by that time, I came to realize that my mom was always in a state of equanimity and peace.

Even when her husband had passed away, she was calm and composed about the whole affair. She shed tears, of course, but she didn't wallow in her grief, and she was back to her normal self after the initial thirteen-day period of mourning that is usual in Indian custom. I found that pretty remarkable.

Then I started to reflect back and realized that my mom, Prem, was never very attached to material things and never got attached to either extremes of life, either of happiness or sadness. If things worked out for us while growing up, great; if they didn't, she would say, "Don't worry. They soon will." Slowly it started to dawn on me that she was the model of a self-realized being, born like so. She clearly didn't do any self-purification work that I was involved in over the past many years. She was born like that, a perfect, simple and happy being of light and unconditional love. It doesn't matter who within my family is not talking to whom at any given time, my mother is the glue. We all have people like that in our families. People everyone like to talk with. People who are above praise or criticism. Beings of love who have no malice or anger or any ego in them. They are just pure love and are here to share more of their love and outright acceptance. I am so proud and humbled by her beautiful demeanor and feel so lucky that she is my mother in this life, who brought me into this world.

Since my dad passed away in 2008, she would tell me, when I would call her from the United States, that she sees my dad often standing in the corner of her room communicating with her. I would laugh such talk of hers away. This was before I had done my research and study of the phenomenon of life after death, physical materializations of discarnate beings, and NDEs that I discuss in the book. Now when she mentions it, I have no doubt she encounters and experiences him somehow. Now my glass is always half full in such matters.

My mother is almost illiterate. She can barely sign her name and practically didn't go to school growing up in her village in India. There were hardly any schools during her childhood, in the late 1920s, in Indian villages.

She is the wisest, humblest, and most loving human being I have met so far in my life. I don't say all this because she is my mom. I acknowledge all this simply because she is a human being I know intimately well. She has always had very few needs, is very accommodative wherever she finds herself in her life, and is thus always happy. Her state of peace and happiness is permanent. She has always been disease free, so far. She learned how to do some basic light yoga postures a while back and some pranayama breathing exercises. She does them regularly, eats moderately, and dances with life effortlessly every day.

Every time I call her, she is laughing about something or the other. What a majestic way to live life—effortlessly, with no conflict within. Everything she encounters flows right through her, and she glides effortlessly, like an eagle through the sky!

I will truly miss her when she is gone. But I know I will be with her again on the other side.

CHAPTER 34

My Physical Transformation

As I started reflecting more on my seemingly automated habitual process, I realized there were many things I was doing just because I had mostly always done them that way. These were my habits. For example, since I grew up in India, I was used to eating wheat roti or nan bread that one eats with North Indian food without realizing the gluten in it was making me fat and also keeping me hungry. I had heard peripherally about the harmful effects of wheat but didn't take them seriously. Then one day I decided to look into this more. Lots of research was available on online as well as in different books. It seemed like everyone knew except me. I thought I'd try to not eliminate but drastically reduce wheat intake. I stopped eating rotis and also changed my cereal to nonwheat. There is no question in my mind that this helped me lose weight and, more important, keep it off. Now I eat my delicious Indian food with rice at Sartaj India Café in Sausalito, one of the best Indian restaurants in Marin.

As I mentioned earlier, I gave up smoking cigars in April 2012 in preparation for my first Vipassana meditation course.

That also reduced my daily intake of the usual one to two glasses of wine I used to drink. By the time I got back from that course, further purified of my mental defilements, I progressively didn't feel the need to have alcohol every day. I had also lost some weight while at the course because of the limited food available during the course. After the course I also realized that my body didn't need as much food as I was throwing in it. My habits had to be watched and understood for them to lose their hold on me. I realized I had an emotional relationship with food. The more I dissolved my conditioning within, the less conflicted and stressed I felt outwardly and the less I felt the need to drink alcohol or overeat to simply compensate for that depleted feeling within.

By the end of 2013, I was barely drinking wine, much less having any other kind of alcohol. Psychologically, I just didn't feel the need for it. I also realized that as I was aging, I had to work that much harder in the gym to keep those extra calories off me that I didn't even feel the need to consume anymore in the first place. Now I drink only socially, if that. It was all about becoming more aware of myself, my habits, and why I was doing what I was doing.

I made some other changes, like not eating fries with my burgers. That got rid of my need to have ketchup, too. I continued to enjoy eating chicken and fish. I had long stopped drinking sodas. I stopped having regular pizzas with my kids, unless I came across a really good one. My kids sometimes drink sodas because their younger, more energetic lifestyles and bodies can process it. As we get older, we forget to shed some of these childhood habits that make us keep gaining weight unnecessarily and often unknowingly.

Since I have a sweet tooth, I substituted one chocolate-brownie Cliff bar per day for the craving to have desserts. Now I don't even crave desserts. I simply warm the bar for thirty seconds in the microwave to allow for the real chocolate within to melt up. So yummy and satisfying.

By becoming more aware of my actions toward myself, each particular habit's hold on me kept progressively lessening, and after some time, they just dissolved. This was no different than my mental defilements, like craving, anger, hate, jealousy, greed, and so forth. Habits are habits. We just need to become fully aware of who we are and what we are doing in our daily living. And that does require a bit of slowing down and stepping back to take stock of our daily unfolding lives and our participation in them.

Healthy eating and living for me really has been that simple. It was less about getting on a particular diet or eating only organic foods or any such need. It was simply watching myself in slow motion to see why I was doing what I was doing on a daily basis. The self-purification work I was deeply immersed in I am sure also helped me do this more easily. It's like the saying, once we get on the right track, everything starts falling into place.

One other point I wanted to add here is that I enjoy dairy, particularly milk (1 percent) during my daily breakfast and an afternoon snack of yogurt.

I also go to the gym pretty regularly, at least five or six times a week. I do a mix of spin classes, one day of rowing ten kilometers in about fifty-five minutes at a resistance of seven, one or two days of CrossFit training, at least a day of forty-five-minute fast-walking on the treadmill, weight lifting a couple of times a week, and about fifteen-to-twenty minutes of physical yoga postures, every time I am in the gym. During my workouts, sometimes I find myself listening to Led Zeppelin and sometimes to Nusrat Fateh Ali Khan, the great Sufi singer from Pakistan, who passed away in 1997.

By making such simple, common-sense changes and having a decent exercise routine, I slowly but progressively lost weight from 2013 to now. Again, my goal was not just to lose weight but to eat better and to clean myself within so I could feel stronger and have more energy available throughout the day. I found that the less conflicted I became within, the more this universal energy coursed through me unobstructed.

I also wanted to make sure my weight loss was gradual so I could keep maintaining it, which I happily have. I went from a bit over 185 pounds on April 1, 2013, to around 173 pounds by the end of June in 2015.

Since then I have lost under a pound, which is great because my goal now is not to lose weight. I am around my threshold weight my body is comfortable with. In this process my waist measurement went from thirty-three to thirty-one, which I have been at since the start of 2015.

I have so much energy and have never felt better in my whole life. I know it is my newfound mental and emotional clarity and freedom as well as my physique.

Frankly, to me it is less important how much I weight but more important how I feel and how much available energy my body can put out and sustain.

Because of my above-mentioned efforts, my body composition changed from April 1, 2013, to the end of June 2015.

On April 1, 2013, I weighed 185.2 pounds based on the InBody 230 scan I had done for free at the Bay Club. The breakdown of this 185.2 number was as follows:

- ° Total body water = 105.8 pounds
- ° Dry lean mass = 39.1 pounds
- ° Body-fat mass = 40.3 pounds

Under body-composition analysis, my skeletal-muscle mass was right at the end of my normal range, but I was told that ideally it should be well past my normal range. My body-fat mass was a bit over my normal range. This number should be ideally under my normal range.

Under what is called the obesity analysis, my BMI (body-mass index) was 25.8, a tad higher than my normal range. My PBF (percentage of body fat) was 21.8, a bit higher than my normal range. The scan indicated that on both of these metrics, I was overweight and needed to lose about fifteen pounds.

So I made all the changes as mentioned above and revisited this machine on June 22, 2015, a little over two years later. My weight was then 173.3 pounds, a reduction of almost twelve pounds. I was easily fitting into a thirty-one waist by then. In the breakdown of this number, my dry lean mass almost stayed the same while my body-fat mass went down to 27.1 pounds. So I reduced my body-fat mass by almost one-third. That was very good, I thought. Also my skeletal-muscle mass was well over my normal range now, which again was as desired and pretty positive. My body-fat mass was now a bit under my normal range, which was also positive.

Lastly, under the obesity analysis, my BMI now was 24.2, still a bit over my normal range, which had shrunk as well, but my PBF was now under my new shrunk range. That was also good news. Overall, the machine this time gave me a passing grade of "normal" versus the last time of "over," implying being overweight then. But it said I still had to lose 1.3 pounds. Apparently our work continues endlessly toward our perfection.

The other important thing I wanted to mention is my eating and sleeping schedule. That also seems to have helped me and thus is worth mentioning here. I regularly have three meals a day and one or two light, healthy snacks between lunch and dinner, which is usually eaten before six in the evening. I am in bed by eight thirty, nine at the latest, and am up by five in the morning. I love to sleep well.

I also became very mindful of the obvious fact that I need my body to operate well so I can get to my goal of self-realization. If my body gets sick for any reason, that will only end up slowing my progress toward my end goal as a lot of my energy would have to get diverted to take care of it now. So once I really started to understand all this obvious stuff, I started looking at my body as my church, my synagogue, my Hindu temple, a sacred place I had to keep clean. This further helped me stop abusing my body with excessive foods, alcohol, and even abusive emotional and sexual relationships.

I started doing yoga in 2007 and since then have really improved in the duration and complexity of physical postures I do. I also realized I could do my yoga postures so much better having less weight around me. The benefits of doing even basic yoga postures is tremendous as has been documented in so many well-written books and medical studies.

One other thing that also shifted how I looked at my body is the National Geographic movie *Incredible Human Machine*. I highly encourage you to watch this or any other available movie about how our incredibly intelligent and amazing human body functions on a daily basis unasked. I am not my body. My body is simply a garment I get to use every time I come to further my learning and growth here on earth.

Since the underlying essence of each one of us is unconditional love, I will share a short story of the Indian restaurant Sartaj that I mention at the start of this chapter. Sartaj was started by Harmail Basi and his dear wife Balbir Basi, twenty years ago in Sausalito. Every year since the opening of the restaurant, they have had a Thanksgiving party in the month of November that is open to one and all. Free food and drinks are available, and a DJ plays Punjabi tunes to dance to till midnight. As the years have passed, and as their dedication to serving the local community has grown, so has the attendance at this yearly party. In 2015, over seven hundred people were provided free food and drinks. Kids, mothers, fathers, and friends pooled their efforts and support, dancing away in the very small space of the restaurant. The spirit of sharing food and love—as I witnessed at the Golden Temple in Amritsar, which I mentioned earlier in the book— was also on full display at the party.

CHAPTER 35

Hatha Yoga and Kundalini
Awakening

ANOTHER IMPORTANT TEXT on yoga, specifically in the Tantra lineage, is *Hatha Yoga Pradipika*, written in the fourteenth century CE in Sanskrit. The aim of this text is the same as that of the other two methodologies or systems already discussed in this book—that of Samadhi or our self-realization. All three are different ways of getting to the same end goal and often share many similar practices of meditation, breath control, and Hatha yoga. Depending on the nature of the yogi, he or she can gravitate to whatever comes more naturally to his or her demeanor.

A good English translation of this book in my mind is, *Asana Pranayama Mudra Bandha* by Swami Satyananda Saraswati, if the reader wants to go deeper into Hatha yoga and its various practices. The book is published by the Bihar school of yoga.

While the four yoga disciplines of karma, Bhakti, Jnana, and Raja yoga and the *Yoga Sutras of Patanjali*, the so-called systems or philosophies, focus more on self-purification efforts of the yogi by the yogi, in my mind Hatha yoga focuses on achieving the same results by the awakening of our Kundalini, which then automatically purifies us from within.

So the yogi's focus in Hatha yoga via different physical postures, pranayama (breathing exercises), and bandhas (collection of life-force energy in specific parts of the physical body by self-closing) is to force release the Kundalini shakti, or energy, lying dormant at the base of our spine.

Once done, the process of Kundalini awakening itself purifies us emotionally, mentally, physically, and spiritually by forcing a new change of perception and outlook in a human being. Kundalini awakening then can be looked at as a raising or elevation of our consciousness within. The human mechanism then desires on its own volition to bring about changes in its thinking and thus outward behaviors.

Hatha in Sanskrit means, sun *(ha)* and moon *(tha)*, or bringing together heat and cold, or the two aspects of our life-force energy, male and female. This union of polarities when achieved at the base of our spine, or at the root chakra, brings about the awakening of our Kundalini shakti lying dormant and coiled in each of us. This Kundalini energy, our seven main chakras, and associated meridian lines exist in our subtle body-energy field.

Though I did not start out on my journey of self-purification through the practices and teachings of the

Hatha Yoga Pradipika, the results are the same. As I have described at various places in the book, my very real experiences with the flow of this energy within me, the constant presence of this energy is unmistakable within each of us once activated by one of many ways.

Gopi Krishna, the local bank manager living near the city of Srinagar in the Jammu and Kashmir state of Northern India, discusses in great detail in his autobiography his painful though amazing experience of accidental Kundalini awakening during his efforts of persistent and deep meditations.

The reason Kundalini awakening can often be very painful in people is if the release of this pent-up energy from the base of our spine manifests through the wrong channel, there apparently can be intense pain experienced by the human organism. There are three main channels (or *nadis*) in the subtle human body that connect the movement of this energy flow between our lower and higher chakras, the Sushumna, or center channel; the Ida, or left channel; and the Pingala, or right channel.

Gopi believed and espoused through his various writings and books that this Kundalini awakening in each of us is our process of higher conscious evolution that is at work in each human being. That Kundalini is the biological reason for our gradual and inherent human-conscious evolution.

Which comes first—our Kundalini awakening that results in our self-realization as Hatha yoga implies or our self-realization that also gets to activate this Kundalini in its flowering? It seems to me a circular loop that feeds on itself, irrespective of how it's triggered, evolving and elevating our human-conscious evolution.

CHAPTER 36

Framework of Our Lives

○ All seven billion people are on the same highway of conscious evolution. Humanity moving slowly but surely up and to the right in each successive generation.

○ It is absolutely possible to accelerate this natural gradual conscious evolution of ours by breaking from the pack to become self-realized in this life. As we saw mentioned earlier by no less than Patanjali in his Yoga Sutras first book discourse, for a one-pointed man, Samadhi is easy to achieve. Once fully awake, we move on to ever higher realms of learning and growth in the spirit world.

○ That sweet water, or love, within tastes the same. It doesn't matter who gets within to taste it, or how or in what way. The key is to get to the ocean and not stay caught in the weeds. At these deeper levels of connection within, outward rituals, forms, and ways of religion or beliefs are transcended.

○ Nothing in our daily lives is happening by chance. Everything is connected and interrelated. We are indeed the architect of our constant unfolding, which unfolds in a way so as to maximize our continued learning.

°   We end up taking our personality as is at the time of death.

So it is imperative that we die well. But to die well, we have to learn to live well. What does living well mean here? To live a life of selfless love, compassion, sharing, caring, and empathy toward one and all. To know in our hearts that we are all one and to live in our daily relationships like that. The more loving and compassionate we become, the more we are able to raise our vibration and the higher the realms in spirit we will get to reside in after this life. The Father indeed has many mansions for different people.

°   Earth is simply a school (like many others) we get to come to purify ourselves and make ourselves a better, cleaner, and shinier version each time. This continued effort on our part results in our self-realization, moksha, or enlightenment.

°   Once the connection within is made by dissolving enough of our conditioning, we become kind, compassionate, humble, loving, selfless, and much more. We don't have to try to be compassionate or humble then. We are that, and these are the attributes of our higher self within. What is sacred in me is also scared in you.

° As I emptied myself of myself, this Source continued to fill me up, ever so more.

Then I truly understood what I had read so many times—that depending on the available emptiness in the vessel—we each allow God to fill us up in that equal proportion.

° It does not matter what version of God we believe in—a personal God, an impersonal God, or no God at all—the purpose of our beliefs, whatever they are and of whichever religion, is to get us to the end, to get to the ocean, to taste this sweet nectar within each of us. The only thing that matters is to get to the end, however one gets there. All paths are leading us to the same place within in union with God as unconditional love.

° Everything is being projected from our inside out. Till we are not able to make the connection with this love or God within, we cannot connect with it outside. Once connected, we see God in everything and everyone.

° Each of us, often not realizing it, is on our own self-propelled karmic journey of self-transformation that forces us to keep adjusting upward in our behavior patterns caused by our daily ups and downs. Once we get to understand this natural unfolding phenomenon, we stop fighting and resisting inevitable changes in our daily lives being presented to us for our own necessary growth.

° We decide on the script, our drama, and its participating actors before coming each time so as to maximize our learning opportunity.

° All of life's efforts of school, work, making money, and relationships can be looked at as necessary outer scaffoldings for the development and completion of the inner structure within each of us. Having served their purpose, all scaffoldings are removed and let go.

° On our spiritual path, it is often not the duration but the intensity, our hunger that produces results.

° There are numerous paths available for us to follow toward our efforts of self-transformation. One is not better than the other. What we get to show for all our efforts, in how we conduct ourselves in our daily encounters—our resultant flowering—is the only thing that matters.

° I am a Hindu, a Muslim, a Christian, a Jew, a Buddhist, and a Sikh. I am a human being.

Daily I do my duty, my dharma, whatever my heart's earnest desire is to achieve. Having done that, I know that in spite of all my efforts, only one door will open, and that's the door I am being guided to go through happily and cheerfully with full acceptance. And I walk through that open door each time.

Appendix

Daily Reflections and Meditations

Monday

- The real purpose of our life is to give and receive love.
- In order to transform others, I first have to transform myself.
- Seek the seeker, which is you, within. (Ramana Maharshi)
- The nature of desire is to stay unfulfilled. (Buddha)
- What we give out (of love, compassion, kindness, hate, or jealousy) we get back.
- Can we be like space that remains untainted by anything that occurs in it? (Buddha)
- For my heart to open, my mind has to open first.
- Be like water—soft, transparent, and malleable.
- Never stay in conflict with anyone. It is wasted energy.
- Life is simply a string of experiences. That's all.
- The opposite of exclude and condemn is include and praise.

Tuesday

- In you I see myself—how can I hate you or hurt you?
- There is nothing wrong with Maya (our world as illusion); enjoy it without identifying with it.
- You must be the change you want to see in the world. (Gandhi)
- The only solution to your problem: *love* more.
- Allow change to happen.
- Nobody can hurt me without my permission. (Gandhi)
- No one likes to be used. Only a wise man feels honored when used because only if you are useful can you be used. (Swami Sukhabodhananda)
- Life is slow subtraction—stay watchful of every passing day.
- Even animals fill their own tummies. Man should do more with himself.
- The more I give of my love unconditionally, the more I receive it.
- It is not enough for me to just love my loved ones—that's easy.
- Whenever you get stuck, go deeper within to release. Keep moving.
- Never accumulate hurt, anger, or a grudge in yourself. Simply sit in meditation to dissolve it.
- Possessive love is limiting and confining. Jealousy and envy breed there.

- ° Can I suspend judgment?
- ° A sure sign of spiritual progress: less Velcro around us.

Wednesday

- ° Can my happiness be dependent on nothing?
- ° Our solution to any given problem in front of us (anger for example) can never be found at the level of the problem; it always has to be at a higher level.
- ° There is a difference between being alone and lonely; find it within.
- ° Life is about experiencing, not accumulating.
- ° Till something is understood, it stays in our thinking as conditioning.
- ° The deeper our experience of love, or God, within, the quieter we become.
- ° Can we live a life with no conflict, and let everything that arises simply pass through us?
- ° Samadhi and our conditioning (ego) have an inverse relationship.
- ° Know that you have come equipped with everything you will ever need within to get to your end, your flowering.
- ° The main reason we can't seem to hold on to our brief ecstatic experiences within is because not enough conditioning has been dissolved yet. As more of our ego is understood and thus

transcended, the longer our blissful and ecstatic experiences get to stay with us.

○ Only an empty cup is useful. Empty yourself of yourself (your ego) to allow God as love to shine through.

○ Seek depth in your life.

○ The cleaner my mind, the faster it's processing, the happier I am.

○ The simple reason we are drawn to unconditional love is because innately that's what we are, each one of us.

Thursday

○ Whenever someone acts in ways that are personally hurtful to me, I remember the times when I myself being more ignorant was probably hurtful toward others. We are all here to learn and grow. When we look through such a lens, we allow personal hurt to simply pass through us.

○ We get to conserve our precious energy when we stay equanimous.

○ Understand your yesterday, and release it.

○ If your answer to my question "When were you happiest?" is "Not now," then conditioning within still needs to be understood and dissolved. Go deeper.

° Detachment (contentment within), equanimity, and unconditional love hang out together. Just catch one. The easiest to catch is equanimity. The hardest, love.

° Can you enjoy the pleasures of the world without getting attached to them? (Tilopa)

° All our conditioning that we are unable to understand and thus dissolve by the time of death, we end up taking with us.

° The more we forgive, the closer we get to love within.

° If you offer no resistance, you encounter no resistance.

° Our hearts cannot open till our minds open first.

° The way to get out of my own way is to have less Velcro around me.

Friday

° The best competition is to compete with myself every day. How can I make myself a better human being today?

° My kindness is the best gift I get to share freely.

° The more I emptied my vessel of my conditioning, the faster I was able to processes incoming data (my constantly unfolding life), and the further it took me on my spiritual path.

° Be like the water, accepting all things that come your way—or like our mother earth.

° This spiritual journey of ours from our head to our heart is the only one worth pursuing.

° Be assured and know that nobody is out to get you.

° I always try to put my best effort toward whatever I want. My effort then releases me from that particular desire, irrespective of the outcome. Then I can move on knowing I tried. The key is to keep moving on.

° Our senses follow our minds. The cleaner the mind is of its conditioning, the easier it is to create distance from our senses (i.e., transcend or detach from them).

° Regardless, keep doing good onto others so you can keep earning merit (i.e., good karma).

° When we don't know what we are missing, we keep missing it.

Weekend

° The more you run away from your fear or anxiety, the more it will follow you around in your relationships.

Understand that fear is not real, it's just an emotion. It simply has to be dissolved each time it is experienced within you. You do this by becoming fully aware of it and not running away from it. Also make sure you are not adding any more fuel, or new energy, to this old sensation of fear that keeps showing up. Just sit and observe your fear each time it shows up. As you do so, its intensity and hold on you will start to diminish. Every psychological fear within us has to be understood and dissolved in such a manner.

° Always let go of former loved ones with love, never with hate or anger. If you let go with hate or anger, you will always keep them with you.

° When someone says or does something that is hurtful to you, ask yourself this question: "What is within me that needs to be healed that is coming up now because of this person's act?" Focus on healing what needs to be healed within you.

° We only generate so much energy every day. Don't waste it by being angry, hateful, jealous, or hurtful toward others or yourself.

° Once I started pointing my finger at myself, I had already done over 50 percent of my spiritual work.

° Our habits breed in our conditioning. The cleaner the mind is of its conditioning, the easier it is to break or dissolve them.

° The freer we become, the less we need.

List of Books I Read in Sequential Order, with Start and Finish Dates

2006

1) *Worldless Wisdom, Celebrating Life and Death* by Swami Sukhabodhananda 08/08/06–08/15/06
2) *The Key* by Cher Huber 11/03/06–11/04/06
3) *Mother Teresa, In the Heart of the World* by Becky Benenate 11/10/06–11/20/06

2007

4) *Bhagavad Gita* by Stephen Mitchell 04/04/07–04/15/07

2008

5) *Autobiography of a Yogi* by SRF 03/13/08–06/16/08

6) *To Be Victorious in Life* by SRF 03/16/08–03/18/08

7) *Spiritual Diary* by SRF 03/19/08–03/22/08

8) *In the Sanctuary of the Soul* by SRF 03/23/08–03/25/08

9) *Man's Eternal Quest* by Sri Sri Parmahansa Yogananda 03/27/08–06/22/08

10) *The Prophet* by Kahlil Gibran 06/06/08–06/07/08

11) *The Bhagavad Gita* by Eknath Easwaran 07/31/08–08/20/08

12) *The Upanishads* by Eknath Easwaran 08/22/08–09/23/08

13) *The Dhammapada* by Eknath Easwaran 11/28/08–12/21/08

14) *Timeless Wisdom* by Eknath Easwaran 10/25/08–11/11/08

15) *The Art of Forgiveness, Loving Kindness and Peace* by Jack Kornfield 12/11/08–12/16/08

16) *The Essential Gandhi* by Louis Fisher 12/24/08–01/02/09

2009

17) *Mohan-Mala: A Gandhian Rosary*, compiled by R K Prabhu 01/05/09–01/11/09

18) *Sayings of Parmahansa Yogananda* by SRF 01/12/09–01/19/09

19) *Parmahansa Yogananda in Memoriam* by SRF 01/19/09–01/22/09
20) *Gandhi the Man: The Story of His Transformation* by Eknath Easwaran 02/01/09–02/14/09
21) *Mother Teresa* by Navin Chawla 02/13/09–02/21/09
22) *The Spiritual Teachings of Ramana Maharshi* 03/24/09–03/30/09
23) *Kundalini: The Evolutionary Energy in Man* by Gopi Krishna 04/03/09–04/09/09
24) *Life After Death* by Deepak Chopra 04/19/09–05/04/09
25) *Ramakrishna and His Disciples* by Christopher Isherwood 05/05/09–05/16/09
26) *Physics of the Soul* by Amit Goswami 05/16/09–05/28/09
27) *The Giving Tree* by Shel Silverstein 07/16/09
28) *Songs of Kabir* translated by Rabindranath Tagore 07/25/09–07/31/09
29) *The Best of Speaking Tree*, volume one 07/25/09–09/18/09
30) *The Essential Teachings of Ramana Maharshi: A Visual Journey* 09/20/09–09/22/09
31) *The Tibetan Book of Living and Dying* by Sogyal Rinpoche 10/20/09–11/17/09
32) *Life After Life* by Raymond Moody Jr. 11/01/09–11/03/09
33) *The Light Beyond* by R. Moody 11/17/09–11/22/09

34) *Closer to the Light* by Melvin Morse with Paul Perry 12/05/09–12/15/09

35) *Reflections on Life after Life* by Raymond Moody 12/15/09–12/18/09

36) *Where God Lives* by Melvin Morse with Paul Perry 12/19/09–01/02/10

2010

37) *Same Souls Many Bodies* by Brain Weiss 01/05/10–01/11/10

38) *Sai Baba, Man of Miracles* by Howard Murphet 01/11/10–01/17/10

39) *Journey of Souls* by Michael Newton 01/17/10–01/26/10

40) *Essential Sufism* by James Fadiman and Robert Frager 01/31/10–02/12/10

41) *The Essential Rumi,* translated by Coleman Barks 02/12/10–02/25/10

42) *Rumi: Bridge to the Soul* by Coleman Barks 02/26/10–03/04/10

43) *The Essential Mystics* by Andrew Harvey 03/04/10–03/14/10

44) *I Heard God laughing* by Daniel Ladinsky 03/20/10–03/23/10

45) *Kabir: Ecstatic Poems* by Robert Bly 03/23/10–03/26/10

46) *The Subject Tonight is Love: 60 Wild and Sweet Poems of Hafiz* by Daniel Ladinsky 03/26/10–03/30/10

47) *The Gospel of Sri Ramakrishna* by Swami Nikhilananda 03/14/10–05/01/10

48) *The Drowned Book, Bahauddin, the Father of Rumi*, translated by Coleman Barks and John Moyne 04/03/10–04/15/10

49) *The Book of Life* by J. Krishnamurti 04/17/10–06/04/10

50) *The First Sikh Spiritual Master: Teachings of Guru Nanak* by Harish Dhillon 05/04/10–05/08/10

51) *Sikhism* by Sewa Singh Kalsi 05/09/10–05/19/10

52) *Life Between Lives* by Michael Newton 05/11/10–05/18/10

53) *On the Road to Freedom* by Swami Paramatmananda 05/19/10–05/24/10

54) *Freedom from the Known* by J Krishnamurti 06/05/10–06/27/10

55) *Voices from the Womb* by Michael Gabriel 06/10/10–06/15/10

56) *Many Lives Many Masters* by Brian Weiss 06/28/10–07/01/10

57) *Only Love is Real* by Brian Weiss 07/02/10–07/06/10

58) *Messages from the Masters* by Brian Weiss 07/06/10–07/15/10

2011

82) *One Thousand Moons: Krishnamurti at Eighty-Five*, texts and photographs by Asit Chandmal 08/31/11

83) *The Soul of Rumi* by Coleman Barks 10/08/11–12/13/11

84) *The Buddha Said...*by OSHO 12/13/11–02/04/12

85) *Destiny of Souls* by Michael Newton 12/27/12–01/29/13

2012

86) *The Great Courses: Buddhism* 01/03/12–02/23/12

87) *Only One Sky: On the Tantric Way of Tilop's Song of Mahamudra* by Shree Rajneesh 02/05/12–02/23/12

88) *The Untethered Soul* by Michael A. Singer 02/23/12–03/01/12

89) *The Real Nature of Mystical Experience* by Gopi Krishna 03/02/12–03/03/12

90) *The Biological Basis of Religion and Genius* by Gopi Krishna 03/03/12–03/09/12

91) *The Riddle of Consciousness* by Gopi Krishna 03/09/12–03/18/12

92) *The Empty Boat: Encounters with Nothingness—Stories of Chuang Tzu* by OSHO 03/31/12–04/30/12

93) *Absolute Tao* by OSHO—*On the Tao Te Ching* by Lao Tzu 05/01/12–05/14/12

94) *Living with Kundalini* by Gopi Krishna 05/23/12–06/07/12

95) *The Second Book of the Tao* by Stephen Mitchell 06/12/12–07/06/12

96) *The Moon Appears When the Water is Still: Reflections of the Dhamma* by Ian McCrorie 06/24/12–06/28/12

97) *Meditation Now, Inner Peace Through Inner Wisdom* by S. N. Goenka 06/28/12–07/05/12

98) *Tao Te Ching,* translated by Gia-Fu Feng and Jane English 06/30/12–07/05/12

99) *Chogyam Trungpa: His Life and Vision* by Fabrice Midal 07/09/12–08/07/12

100) *The Dalia Lama's Secret Temple,* texts by Ian A. Baker, photographs by Thomas Laird 08/07/12–08/19/12

101) *Masters of Mahamudra* by Keith Dowman 08/28/12–10/17/12

102) *Rabia: The Mystic and Her Fellow Saints in Islam* by Margaret Smith 10/18/12–11/15/12

103) *The Gift: Poems by* Hafiz, translated by Daniel Ladinsky 11/25/12–12/15/12

104) *Dying to Be Me* by Anita Moorjani 12/18/12–12/23/12

105) *John of God: The Brazilian Healer Who's Touched the Lives of Millions* by Heather Cumming and Karen Leffler 12/20/12–01/05/13

106) *Proof of Heaven* by Eben Alexander
12/23/12–12/26/12

2013

107) *A Book of Psalms* by Stephen Mitchell
01/09/13–01/13/13
108) *And Life Goes On* by Francisco Candido Xavier
01/13/13–01/18/13
109) *Chico Xavier: Medium of the Century* by Guy
Lyon Playfair 01/19/13–01/24/13
110) *Women in the Praise of the Sacred*, edited by
Jane Hirshfield 01/26/13–02/03/13
111) *The Flying Cow* by Guy Lyon Playfair 01/28/13–
02/11/13
112) *The Enlightened Mind* by Stephen Mitchell
02/11/13–03/03/13
113) *Spiritual Journeys: Visiting John of God* by Gail
Thackray's 03/05/13–03/09/13
114) *Sharafuddin Maneri: The Hundred
Letters (Classics of Western Spirituality)*
03/10/13–05/06/13
115) *Farid ad-Din Attar's Memorial of God's
Friends (Classics of Western Spirituality)*
05/07/13–07/24/13
116) *Third Eye Open* by Susan Reintjes
07/25/13–08/03/13

117) *The Conference of the Birds* by Farid Attar
08/05/13–08/10/13

118) *Small Mediums at Large* by Terry Iacuzzo
08/21/13–08/29/13

119) *The Infinite Boundary* by Guy Lyon Playfair
09/08/13–10/16/13

120) *Spirit Teachings* by William Stainton Moses
09/27/13–10/28/13

121) *30-Second Religion,* editor Russell Re Manning
10/16/13–10/26/13

122) *More Spirit Teachings* by William Stanton Moses
11/29/13–12/07/13

123) *Jesus and the Essenes* by Dolores Cannon
12/07/13–12/14/13

124) *They Walked with Jesus* by Dolores Cannon
12/14/13–12/21/13

125) *Between Death and Life* by Dolores Cannon
12/21/13–12/30/13

126) *The Enlightened Heart* by Stephen Mitchell
12/30/13–01/01/14

2014

127) *The Gospel According to Jesus* by Stephen Mitchell 01/01/14–01/07/14

128) *Ramana Maharshi and the Path of Self Knowledge* by Arthur Osborne 01/14/14–02/03/14

129) *Missionaries of the Light* by Francisco Candido Xavier 02/03/14–02/19/14

130) *The Bhagavad Gita,* translated by Juan Mascaro 02/05/14–02/07/14

131) *Thomas Merton: The Inner Experience* 02/19/14–02/20/14

132) *Vasisthas Yoga* by Swami Venkatesananda 03/19/14–05/29/15

133) *The Book of Miracles: The Healing Work of Joao de Deus* by Josie Ravenwing 05/29/14–06/06/14

134) *The Upanishads,* translated by Juan Mascaro 05/30/14–06/02/14

135) *Arigo: Surgeon of the Rusty Knife* by John G Fuller 06/09/14–06/12/14

136) *The Miracle Man: The Life story of Joao de Deus* by Robert Pellegrino-Estrich 06/13/14–06/15/14

137) *A Journal of the Mystery of Uri Geller* by Andrija Puharich 06/17/14–06/24/14

138) *Healing Hands* by J. Bernard Hutton 06/24/14–06/27/14

139) *The Two Worlds of Helen Duncan* by Glen Brealey 06/28/14–07/01/14

140) *Dimensions of Enchantment* by Manfred Cassirer 07/01/14–07/04/14

141) *The Dhammapada* by Juan Mascaro 07/02/14–07/03/14

142) *Spiritual Realization: Inner Values in Everyday Life,* communicated to Ivy Northage by her spiritual guide, Chan 07/04/14–07/13/14

143) *While I Remember: The Life Story of Ivy Northage*, edited by Brenda Marshall 07/14/14–07/21/14

144) *The Spirit Within*, Chan through the trance mediumship of Ivy Northage 07/23/14–08/05/14

145) *More Wisdom of Ramadahn*, through the Mediumship of Ursula Roberts 08/06/14–08/15/14

146) *Living in Two Worlds: The autobiography of Ursula Roberts* 08/16/14–08/25/14

147) *Journey Beyond*, trance talks by Chan, spirit guide of Ivy Northage 08/26/14–08/28/14

148) *Miracles of the Bible* by Manfred Cassirer 08/27/14–09/13/14

149) *Wisdom of Ramadahn*, through the mediumship of Ursula Roberts 09/14/14–10/03/14

150) *Devotees Speak, Shree Sai baba of South San Francisco* by Gwyn McGee 09/30/14–10/01/14

151) *The Life and Teachings of Sai Baba of Shirdi* by Antonio Rigapoulos 10/04/14–11/08/14

152) *The Bijak of Kabir* by Linda Hess and Sukhdev Singh 11/08/14–11/20/14

153) *Bharosha Ma: 22 Weeks with Divinity* by Gwyn McGee 11/21/14–11/24/14

154) *Shankara's Crest—Jewel of Discrimination* by Swami Prabhavananda and Christopher Isherwood 11/25/14–12/03/14

155) *The Sermon on the Mount According to Vedanta* by Swami Prabhavananda 12/03/14–12/11/14

156) *How to Know God: The Yoga Aphorisms of Patanjali* by Swami Prabhavananda and Christopher Isherwood 12/12/14–12/27/14

157) *Alec Harris: The Full Story of his Remarkable Physical Mediumship* by Louie Harris 12/27/14–01/05/15

2015

158) *Beyond the Himalayas* by Murdo MacDonald-Bayne 01/06/15–01/20/15

159) *The Thirteen Petalled Rose* by Adin Steinsaltz 01/22/15–01/25/15

160) *9 1/2 Mystics* by Herbert Weiner 01/26/15–02/05/15

161) *The Light and Fire of the Baal Shem Tov* by Yitzhak Buxbaum 02/06/15–02/19/15

162) *A History of God* by Karen Armstrong 02/20/15–03/05/15

163) *The Life and Teachings of Hillel* by Yitzhak Buxbaum 03/07/15–03/13/15

164) *The Way of the Servant, Living the Light of Christ, Enlightenment: The Final Stage*, as given through Jayem 03/11/15–03/12/15

165) *Song of Songs* by Jeanne Guyon 03/13/15–03/15/15

166) *Religion in Practice* by Swami Prabhavananda 03/15/15–03/23/15

167) *Ecstatic Spontaneity: Saraha's Three Cycles of Doha* by Herbert Guenther 03/28/15–04/7/15

168) *50 Jewish Messiahs* by Jerry Rabow 04/08/15–04/12/15

169) *No God but God* by Reza Aslan 04/12/15–04/26/15

170) *Zealot: The Life and Times of Jesus of Nazareth* by Reza Aslan 04/27/15–05/09/15

171) *On the Mystical Shape of the Godhead* by Gershom Scholem 05/10/15–05/23/15

172) *The World Within* by J. Krishnamurti 05/24/15–06/09/15

173) *Knocking at the Open Door* by R. E. Mark Lee 06/09/15–06/16/15

174) *Immortals by My Side* by Rosemary Brown 06/16/15–06/22/15

175) *The Unconditioned Mind* by David Edmund Moody 06/23/15–06/26/15

176) *Mind to Mind: The Secrets of Your Mind Energy Revealed* by Betty Shine 06/27/15–07/05/15

177) *A Vision of the Sacred: My Personal Journey with Krishnamurti* by Sunanda Patwardhan 07/06/15–07/12/15

178) *Ena Twigg: Medium* 07/13/15–07/24/15

179) *The Tapestry of Life*, compiled by Marjorie Aarons 07/24/15–07/28/15

180) *The Other Side: An Account of My Experiences with Psychic Phenomena* by Bishop James A. Pike and Diane Kennedy 07/28/15–08/05/15

181) *The Meaning of Mary Magdalene* by Cynthia Bourgeault 08/06/15–08/17/15

182) *The Guru's Gift: A Kundalini Awakening* by Ruth Angela 08/17/15–08/23/15

183) *The Little Book of Hercules* by William Bodri 08/31/15–09/13/15

184) *The Swan in the Evening* by Rosamond Lehmann 09/14/15–09/15/15

185) *The Awakening Letters: Varieties of Spiritual Experiences in the Life after Death* by Cynthia Sandys and Rosamond Lehmann 09/18/15–09/26/15

186) *Stalking the Wild Pendulum* by Itzhak Bentov 09/26/15–10/06/15

187) *One Mind* by Larry Dossey 10/07/15–10/15/15

188) *Paranormal: My Life in the Pursuit of the Afterlife* by Raymond Moody and Paul Perry 10/21/15–10/23/15

189) *The Legend of Baal Shem* by Martin Buber 10/25/15–10/30/15

190) *Supernormal* by Dean Radin 11/02/15–11/07/15

191) *Hasidic Spirituality for a New Era: The Religious Writings of Hillel Zeitlin* by Arthur Green 11/07/15–11/10/15

192) *Self-Knowledge (Atmabodha)* by Swami Nikhilananda 11/19/15–11/21/15

193) *The Gift of Healing* by Ambrose A. Worrall & Olga Worrall 11/22/15–12/01/15

2016

List of Recommended DVDs

1) *I Am,* directed by Tom Shadyac
2) *What the Bleep Do We Know*
3) *Incredible Human Machine* by National Geographic
4) *The Wisdom of Bhagavad Gita*, a talk by Brother Anandamoy, SRF
5) *Understanding Karma*, a talk by Brother Anandamoy, SRF
6) *Dhamma Discourses* by S. N. Goenka—Goenka's daily evening discourses from a ten-day Vipassana meditation course, available at pariyatti.org
7) *Mother Teresa*, a film by Ann and Jeanette Petrie with narration by Richard Attenborough
8) *Mother Teresa: The Legacy*, a film by Ann and Jeanette Petrie
9) *Gandhi*, a movie about Mahatma Gandhi and his legacy
10) *Awake: The Life of Yogananda*, a movie about Yogananda and SRF

11) *Healing*, a documentary about John of God and the workings of the Casa

12) *Astral City*, a movie based on the famous book *Nosso Lar* through Chico Xavier

13) *The Letters*, a movie about Mother Teresa of Calcutta, her formative years, and early work in India

14) *Doing Time, Doing Vipassana*—A Israeli documentary film by two women filmmakers, Ayelet Menahemi and Eilona Ariel, shot primarily at Tihar Jail, New Delhi highlighting the benefits of a ten-day Vipassana meditation course on prison inmates, available at pariyatti.org

15) *Into Great Silence*, directed by Philip Groning—A movie about daily living of the Carthusian monks and their Catholic order of eleventh century CE

Endnotes

Introduction

[1] Gibran, *The Prophet*, page 52

[2] Henri-Charles Puech, et al., *The Gospel According to Thomas*, Harper & Row 1959

Chapter 4: Eknath Easwaran

[1] Kamat.com

Chapter 8: Gandhi

[1] Brainyquote.com

[2] *Gandhi*, the movie

Chapter 9: Ramana Maharshi

[1] *Maharshi: The Spiritual Teachings of Ramana Maharshi*, Shambhala Classics, foreword by C.G. Jung, Page xiv

[2] *Maharshi, The Essential Teachings of Ramana Maharshi, A Visual Journey*, edited by Matthew Greenblatt, page 20

[3] Ibid., page 20

[4] Ibid., page 94

[5] Ibid., page 66

Chapter 10: Kabir

1   Poemhunter.com: Are you looking for me
2   Tagore, *Songs of Kabir*, page xiii–xiv
3   Hess and Sukhdev, *The Bijak of Kabir*, page 31
4   Ibid., 128

Chapter 12: The Sufis Mystics, Drunk with Love of God

1   Ladinsky, *Love Poems from God*, page 2
2   Ibid., page 11

Chapter 24: Communications from the Spirit World

1   Henri-Charles Puech, et al., *The Gospel According to Thomas*, Harper & Row 1959

Chapter 26: Mahamudra Teachings

1   Dowman, *Masters of Mahamudra*, page 12

Chapter 32: Karma and Reincarnation

1   Dossey, *One Mind*, xxi
2   Schopenhauer, *Parerga and Paralipomena*, page 368

About the Author

SUDEEP BALAIN IS a life coach, energy healer, and portfolio manager who has worked on both the buy and sell sides of Wall Street, in New York, and in San Francisco. Before his career on Wall Street, Sudeep worked in senior marketing positions at semiconductor companies in Silicon Valley for ten years.

Sudeep earned his MBA from Southeastern Louisiana University in 1988 and his bachelor's in electronics engineering from Thapar Institute of Engineering and Technology (TIET) in Patiala, India, in 1985.

He currently lives in Mill Valley with his three children, Rohan, Arkin, and Samara.

You Are Love is his first book.

To contact Sudeep visit his website, www.sudeepbalain. com.

You Are Love

Sudeep Balain